Doorways of Grace

My Uncommon Journey to Healing, Wholeness and Meeting Jesus

Tracy Gatewood

Parson's Porch & Company

Parson's Porch Books

Doorways of Grace: My Uncommon Journey to Healing, Wholeness and Meeting Jesus

ISBN: Softcover 978-1508952152

Copyright © 2015 by Tracy Gatewood

All rights reserved. No part of this book may be reproduced or transmitted in any form or by any means, electronic or mechanical, including photocopying, recording, or by any information storage and retrieval system, without permission in writing from the publisher.

Cover Design Credit: Allison P. Adams and Nancy C. Mauck

To order additional copies of this book, contact:

Parson's Porch Books
1-423-475-7308
www.parsonsporch.com

Parson's Porch Books is an imprint of Parson's Porch & Company (PP&C) in Cleveland, Tennessee. PP&C is an innovative non-profit organization which raises money by publishing books of noted authors, representing all genres. All donations from contributors and profits from publishing are shared with the poor.

Doorways of Grace

Acknowledgements

The reasons for writing this book were to offer hope to people that are walking through seasons of uncommon difficulties, as well as to raise awareness of God's goodness and mercy through trial and to gain a better understanding of Jesus through the lens of my own personal journey.

I wish to extend a special note of gratitude to the following-

Jesus Christ, who is all Grace and all Truth. You gave your life so I would have one forever. All words of gratitude are inadequate for a sacrifice of this magnitude but Thank You.

Barbara S. White, my best friend and sole (soul) sounding board. Thank you for your kindness, hospitality and friendship to me for over fifteen years.

To my Pastors ~ your ministries were brought to me by the Lord in the perfect time and season that they were needed. Your individual teachings have had an indelible impact and influence on my life. Thank you, thank you for answering the call of God on your life.

Lastly, to a few special people that God strategically positioned into my life over the years, just when I needed them to walk through the door: Allie Beth Allman, Suzanne White, Pat Caven and Charlie and Patty Renfroe. The intersecting of our lives has had an impact on me in ways that you could never truly know. Thank you.

Table of Contents

Chapter 1	*In the Beginning*	11
Chapter 2	*Pouring the Foundation*	21
Chapter 3	*A Closed Door, An Opened Stain Glass Window*	35
Chapter 4	*The Power of Healing Prayer*	48
Chapter 5	*A Supernatural Season*	57
Chapter 6	*Good is the Enemy of Best*	66
Chapter 7	*God's Timing is Never Late*	78
Chapter 8	*The Perfect Storm*	90
Chapter 9	*It is God's Will for You to Prosper*	103
Chapter 10	*Mercy Triumphs Over Judgment*	111
Chapter 11	*It is Finished – Keep Your Eyes on Jesus*	117

Introduction

This book is a very personal account of my 17 year grace filled journey in meeting Jesus, beginning first with an understanding of God as a loving Father, then meeting Holy Spirit and finally through a revelatory encounter that forever galvanized my relationship with the beautiful Son Himself. Through separation then divorce due to spouse's sexual addiction, a career change from business owner to ministry staffer, high income to near poverty, then moving from a dynamic Southern city to a tornado torn Alabama college town, each one of these situations played an important role in the experience.

It is my desire to show how a gracious and loving Father led through a series of wide open doors and supernatural seasons in which I badly needed things to happen that only He could do. Following several seasons of traumatic trial and testing, He placed me on a path to healing, hope and restoration. He did it for me and He will do it for you. You can be free of fear; learning to lean with confidence on your best friend and very own internal transformational leader; God's Holy Spirit. Listening to the Spirit coupled with the disciplines of study, daily worship and intercessory prayer have greatly enriched my life and brought it to a higher dimension in understanding the Godhead.

The crown of thorns that was placed on Jesus' head prior to His crucifixion drew blood from a Deity, purchasing our covenant right as believers to emotional health and a sound, stable mind. His blood has afforded us the ability, through the Holy Spirit's power, to be free of chronic fear and anxiety, condemnation, and depression or any other emotionally damaging condition. Emotional and physical freedoms were both purchased at the cross. Every person consecrated to God through His Son has been guaranteed the right and the ability to possess a mind calibrated to Jesus' own mind. God is Jehovah Shalom. Shalom is defined as peace and wholeness, prosperity and welfare, one only needs to know how to access His peace and rest.

God is full of mercy and has great love for you. Jesus has set you free. Live free.

Tracy L. Gatewood

Chapter One

In the Beginning

And they overcame him because of the blood of the Lamb and because of the word of their testimony, and they did not love their life even when faced with death. Revelation 12:11

I was a late bloomer in knowing Jesus. As a child, I grew up attending church every Sunday, sitting there week after week believing that I had everything necessary to get to Heaven when it was my time "to pass". I never liked that term and still don't. In reality, I was sitting in church, week after week, with no understanding that there was such a thing as a true and active relationship with God through Jesus. I sat in church for years as a youth and young adult believing I would glide successfully through "The Pearlies" with no hesitation. I was wrong.

In college and throughout my early 20's, I steered clear of churches but at 28 moved to Atlanta for a job as an Assistant Marketing Director for a regional shopping center. My performance-based identity had found its sweet spot. The Marketing Director, another Assistant Marketing Director and the Event Coordinator were all let go in a departmental purging six weeks after I was hired, leaving me and the secretary to work 70 – 80 hour weeks. During a time of bleary eyed exhaustion, deciding it was time to seek a more balanced existence, I walked 1 block to a church that shared their parking lot with my neighbors and was the largest Presbyterian assembly in the country. I had grown up in that denomination so this choice felt comfortable, not to mention, you could not beat the convenience factor.

The Senior Pastor was a beloved older gentleman and great communicator of masterfully crafted moral essays that made my sharp young mind really think about moral virtue, where I was headed and why, yet he rarely mentioned Jesus. I did not miss this because I knew little more about Jesus than what a flannel graph or stained glass window would depict. It is a truth that God meets people where they are and having a place to meet for church on Sundays to hear a grandfatherly pastor suited my needs well, anything more would have turned me off and sent me away. At this point in my early thirties, I held a laser focus on my career and on making my mark on the Atlanta business scene. All of my efforts were concentrated on networking and making contacts and building relationships that would forward my career. God was nowhere in the picture and it definitely never occurred to me that a relationship with Him could assist my career. I intersected with God only one day per week with the rest of my days working and striving diligently in my small company with little knowledge or true understanding of Jesus and absolutely no knowledge of the Holy Spirit except to recite his name in the *Apostles' Creed*. You know…"conceived by the Holy Spirit, born of the Virgin Mary, suffered under Pontius Pilate - that *Apostles' Creed*.

At the age of 31, after two and a half years of working 70 hour weeks, managing a marketing department for a million square foot plus shopping center I was still earning a salary of less than $30,000 because the previous regime had left a significant budget deficit. I decided it was time to launch out and start my own endeavor based in the reasoning that owning a successful business would set me on a trajectory that would provide everything needed in my life. Over a short period, through hard work and a focused mind, I acquired coveted Atlanta-based industry accounts and was moving along an enviable career path. Content in my singleness, business-related matters and little else held my full attention.

In the fall of 1993, two friends asked me to meet a man that was their longtime friend but I paid little attention to their requests for a set up until one day, I finally relented. He was a quiet, kind, and reserved man a few years older that came from a family that were committed church attenders. It was important for me to marry someone that went to church – but because of where I was in my faith, I was not particular which one, as long as it was Christian and preferably not too terribly fundamental. I was accustomed to churches with plenty to recite in a unified, corporate atmosphere, and those that shied away from teaching Jesus or using name tags of any sort. In these churches it was easy to come and go and no one knew who I was or knew my personal business nor did they appear to care. God, preached from these pulpits, was non-threatening in its subject matter; ethereal, untouchable and always way "up there" somewhere in the holy other. Accepting and understanding Jesus was a different matter and level of faith entirely, as I would one day learn.

My relationship with this man strengthened quickly, built

on an unhealthy foundation as it would be between two people that were viewing relationships through very fractured, even shattered lenses. Within 7 months we were engaged and at 33, rationalizing that I had gleaned all of the necessary information after waiting that long to marry, convinced myself that it was time to take the leap. All of my friends were married and I truly cared for him and believed that he was the right person at the right time but doing so unknowingly, making these determinations through the lens of an unbeliever.

Just a month following my acceptance of his proposal, my prospective groom moved to a small coastal town to begin his new job and prepare for my move south which I had agreed to do but doing so kicking and screaming from my beloved city of Atlanta. I had greatly enjoyed the activities and offerings of this large city – we were total opposites in this regard and several others. My business needed to continue to operate and the distance would make things very difficult, how we were going to make ends meet was never fully addressed and an uncertainty and my business had consistently provided stable income. Being a Type A, intelligent and self- sufficient female, moving away from all apparent financial security to a small coastal town where I could not even find an office supply store defied all logic but believing that it was part of my new role as a wife, I began making all the proper preparations to leave. This was an entirely new experience on life's journey as I had trusted in my own skill, experience and instincts throughout my adulthood.

Our spiritual life, if you can say we had one, was split

between two churches; one his family attended in a nearby city and one that we found on our own that was not quite as straight-laced, and was smaller with more of a coastal flavor. There was still no movement toward anything that was drawing me into a closer relationship with God, or Jesus. We did not develop any deep relationships at either place but that was a function of where we were in our walk and not the fault of the churches.

One day early on in our marriage, his job ended abruptly because the new company with which he had taken a position was undercapitalized and was going out of business. This job transition opened the door for a reassessment of our location. Rather than move to the nearby large city, we had an opportunity to move to another city located between Atlanta and a large, metropolitan city in Alabama. This meant I was only 1.5 hours from Atlanta and he just an hour from where he could find a solid job. I proceeded to cultivate and grow my marketing business in Atlanta. We were not spending a great deal of time together which was beginning to cause friction but we were working through it.

Suddenly, and again, his job ended and we were met with yet another choice of where to move. My business was performing very well with important shopping center and trade show accounts yielding a high industry profile so consequently it was becoming more and more challenging for me to live away from Atlanta. The decision was made to return which was met with immediate relief on my part. We had no church in this timeframe of our marriage and I was working non-stop with a large staff and living an hour and a half away. He was very reluctant to return back to Atlanta, for reasons he would not clearly articulate, but my income was what we had to depend on at that time, so we returned.

Despite the intense work pace, not long after returning to Atlanta, I began to notice a turn in behavior – most notably, lengthy unexplained absences. There had been some unexplained lapses of time in his whereabouts while living in the coastal town – the other location was harder to track because we were both traveling. There had been question marks in my mind about this but my business was becoming increasingly more challenging with additional staff and projects and it was all consuming. My focus on my business was distracting me from focusing on my marriage and in retrospect (which this entire book is written from) I understand that my priorities were out of alignment at this point in my marriage.

One weekend his parents drove into Atlanta for a visit and he said that he needed to leave and asked me to stay at the house to entertain them. Frustrated, I pressed hard to know where he was going …. this time. He became quite emotional and explained that he was going to a meeting because he was having some issues and there were people helping him through them. I pressed for more information but just as I was doing so his parents walked in and then he left for his "mystery meeting". Our return to Atlanta in 1996 became the beginning of the end of our marriage although it took 3 additional years for the nails to be hammered into the coffin.

Later that year, he was let go from another job with no real explanation for the separation from the employer. Because he could not find a job, he stepped into work for my company as the manager of the business which eventually created resentment on both sides making the situation even worse. It seemed that this further financially dependent state, plus working for his wife although in a management capacity, was sparking anger and passive aggressive behavior.

Throughout 1997, the marriage continued sliding then spiraling as finances became tighter, absences became more frequent and I continually refused to get down to the bottom of the problem to mine for or even ask the right questions. We never had a joint checking account throughout the marriage which was by his choice, and never mine. The obvious issues were simply not being dealt with until one day in early February 1998, while working on a project for a regional shopping center I had worked a very long day, capping off a very long week. When I returned, he was not home. When he came in, he had no real explanation of where he had been and I continued to press for an answer but to no avail. The next day passed, and late that afternoon I said that it was time for us to have a conversation and we sat down in the den at 6:00 PM. Again, pressing for answers, he began to weep, and then sobbing stated that he had a sexual addiction, and had had one for a very long time. Stunned I asked, "How long has this been going on? "Before our marriage? " The answer was yes, "So, is this with other people – are you having sex with other people?" He waffled but said yes and began to weep. "So, about how many times have you done this since we have been married.... 75, 100?" I asked this somehow jokingly, anything to break the tension and not expecting it to be more than a few. His response confirmed an answer that totally stunned me. Apparently, my husband had convinced himself that moving away from Atlanta, rife with fellow sex addicts, and returning to his hometown, plus having a new bride would free him from the deep pain and tormenting thoughts that are all part and parcel of the sexual addiction package. This assumption turned out to be a very dangerous, damaging and traumatic decision at my expense.

Shaken with emotion, he rose from the sofa and walked upstairs, and five minutes later was walking back down the stairs with a large pre- packed overnight bag, announcing that he would be living with his "Sponsor" for several weeks. He then turned and walked out the kitchen door into the garage and left. Unable to move, I remained frozen in the same chair staring out into the den, finally rising and heading for bed at 3 AM. I did not hear from him for several days and made no attempts at contact, not knowing what I would say if I did reach him. My life had been going 100 mph and had now crashed into a brick wall.

Totally broken, I continued to try to operate my business but was barely accomplishing simple day to day tasks well and finally found it necessary to turn the daily responsibilities over to my manager. For months into years I had been blaming myself for the difficulties and strain in the marriage. All of this reality began crashing in wave after wave, as I began to process the magnitude and depth of this lengthy betrayal. Believing that something was wrong with me because he was not attracted to me as his wife and condemning myself when all the while he was having illicit experiences outside of the marriage. The revelation of his promiscuity turned every aspect of my life completely upside down.

The following day we experienced severe storms and heavy rains across the Atlanta region. After hours of deluge the basement began to flood. I walked downstairs to find the Wet Vac and to begin the work of pulling the water from the carpet. As I began processing the magnitude of the previous night's conversation, something broke within me and I began to bang the hose on the ground, jerking it back as hard as I could over and over again, sucking up the water while sobbing until totally exhausted from the labor. Emotionally drained, I continued to see more and more of the reality of the magnitude of what had just been revealed to me, and its traumatic impact began to seep into my soul. I walked upstairs, totally spent, getting into bed alone, and marking a season of many, many months of being alone with God in our home.

PERSPECTIVE

If you are ready to marry, ask the Lord to bring to you His best and wait on His perfect timing to reveal the person that He has prepared for you. Remember, God put Adam to sleep and took a rib from his side to make Eve, Adam was not out searching the garden for a wife, and God made Eve for Adam and brought her to him. Remember, too, Eve was not perfect even though God made Eve for Adam from Adam. She did not trust God and disobeyed His command. We are all given free will yet must never use our free will to choose disobedient acts that are harmful to our spouses.

Chapter Two
Pouring the Foundation

Several weeks prior to his confession, I had signed up for a seminar that was to be held the upcoming weekend. The title was "God, The Divine Romancer". I drug myself over to the church to attend the seminar which was only a few days after he had left the house. Angry, and shattered, and not good company to anyone I felt that God wanted me to go and I was correct. The seminar's keynote was a woman unknown to me at the time that was part of a powerful Christian duo operating a ministry specializing in relational wholeness and sexual brokenness. At the close of the seminar, I gave a brief rundown of what had happened and asked to meet with her for counsel. Our counseling relationship lasted 1.5 years. She gave me insights into the world of people that struggled in the same area of my husband that I am convinced would have remained undiscovered, thereby hindering my healing journey.

God had pre-ordained our meeting to intersect right at the exact time that it would become necessary – the opening of a *doorway of grace*. In addition, two wonderful women sat next to me at this seminar, one of whom remains a dear friend even today. My counselor's acute discernment throughout our meeting times remained very strong. She continually used the time to train me to focus on myself, how I was managing the process and to look at what was happening in my own heart. She only allowed me to focus on his actions just briefly before she would move me away from those feelings and back onto me – only a very short "blame timeframe" was ever allowed. We spent months walking back through my childhood and down roads and trails that I had never dealt with introspectively. Without making me feel condemned or wrong, she helped me to unravel how I could make a choice of marrying someone that could never love me in a way that a true female in a God-centered relationship needed to experience love from a truly healthy male.

For the future of my relational health, it was imperative to replace the shattered lenses with which I had been viewing dating and marital relationships with a clear pair of healed lenses. This began with learning that I had a true identity in Christ and one I needed to discover. Equally important, was to understand the depth and height of love that God has for me as well as recognize the needs that God created within me as a woman. She prayed over me every session in Spirit-filled prayers that I had never heard spoken. My counselor and her husband founded and ran a program that exists to work with cases of sexual brokenness and healing. Together they have been responsible for saving lives and marriages of countless numbers of people. God was so gracious to order my steps to meet them in just the perfect timing to bring clarifying information to everything that I was experiencing.

One of the primary redeeming factors of this personal tragedy was that it brought me totally to the end of myself, while providing insights and revelation into God in ways in which I had never understood Him before.

Many well-known evangelists and teachers accepted Christ in their early teens. I will always wonder how the Lord would have used my life had I been more focused on Him from a very early age. I would have avoided many painful, personal landmines had I been more knowledgeable in His Word, and held a more deeply rooted level of trust in who He is and His goodness and Fatherly love towards me.

In early 1998, at the age of 37, I began visiting a women's Bible study that met in Buckhead, one in which I had attended sporadically upon returning from Alabama several years earlier. Recognizing that I was in way over my head with what was happening in my personal life, I needed to be around biblical teaching, and Christian people, but did not want to explain the personal details of what was happening in my marriage to anyone. This was the first real fellowship group that I ever attended as an adult in a church setting. Week after week I attended this group and sat in a chapel of 200 women listening to one speaker after another. As each session ended, we would disperse and go on about the rest of our week, living our private lives still, well …. privately. This suited me just perfectly, or so I thought. Aside from the "Wet Vac" day, I had not shed another tear over what was happening but knew that there was a tremendous backlog of emotion that was being stuffed down which was starting to impact my disposition – hopelessness is hard to hide on a person.

One morning at one of these weekly bible study sessions, a speaker was describing a book that he had written about a tragic incident somewhere in the U.S. – and to this day, I do not know exactly what he said that triggered this but I began to cry, and then started sobbing uncontrollably. I simply could not stop – I cried and cried, losing it in front of all these well-coiffed women strangers. It was as if a cork had popped out of a bottle and although completely mortified, I could not do anything to keep my grief from flowing out! The speaker started staring, and every woman in the room looked at me like I was a nut – the lay leaders had no idea how to handle it and most were too embarrassed for me themselves and would not take the initiative to approach me, as this was just a little too transparent for this group.

When I left that day, I never returned, not because I lost it, but because God clearly revealed that this was not the type of environment needed to support me through this season, nor one that could facilitate the type of healing required to bring forth restoration. Had this experience not occurred, with all of its discomfort and embarrassment, I could have settled for ankle deep environments lacking in authenticity and transparency, while missing the deep wells of love, acceptance, and grace that God wanted to show me during this time. I was right; He had more – much more to show. He wanted me to discover and then drill down into just the right well to be found by His leading.

A large Baptist church was just down the road from my Dunwoody home. I had been told of two gifted young pastors that were using this church facility until the church for one of them was completed further north. I was desperate for solid teaching and for anything that would help me make sense of what was happening and these pastors were very gifted teachers and communicators that brought a new relevancy to the bible that I had never heard preached. They actually were teaching entire sermons from the bible and interpreting verses and explaining to people in plain English what it meant. Remarkable! Not moral essays! Without knowing anyone else that regularly attended, I went to this church week after week, and continued to press harder to understand God's word and to learn as much as I could about Him.

In the spring of 1998, I truly accepted Jesus as my Savior and was immediately formally baptized in an Elder's swimming pool. Although christened as a child, I consider the age of 37 to be my age of salvation because this was when I clearly understood the meaning of my decision. All the rest of that day and evening, I felt as if I had been dry cleaned from the inside out and guess in a sense had been– this type of supernatural cleansing can only come through this experience. You know what it feels like to have your teeth cleaned and not wanting to eat anything afterward to clutter them up? That is how I felt about my whole body after being baptized. I purchased my first cross necklace and wore it proudly – feeling like it gave me new credibility or something which of course it did not. I wanted people to notice it like a great big neon sign shouting, "She's Different Now. She's Accepted Jesus Christ!" and of course, just the opposite is true. You are different, and you hope people notice and that they want what you have, but it takes much more than a piece of jewelry to accomplish that objective.

God was downloading to me all kinds of revelation during this new season. I saw that attending church once per week was important but there was so much more depth to

Christianity. Even up through my twenties and into my thirties, I did not see that I was in danger of not being received into Heaven. Now through the mature mind of an adult, able to grasp the revelation that Jesus had paid for all of my sin debt, I could see how I had been missing everything. For me growing up, accepting the belief that Jesus was the son of God was never an obstacle – it was never a stretch for me to believe that Jesus had returned to earth as God's Son to walk out a life that illustrated who His Father was so that people would know and understand they had a Father in Heaven that created them for His love. The acceptance of Jesus as God's Son came easily and I thought that was everything necessary to claim fire insurance to steer clear of hell. But once I understood the concept of His holiness, and that Jesus willingly gave His life of His own volition for me to live eternally– that carried much more weight and with it, a much greater desire to give back to the Lord and His kingdom. My understanding of the exchange that occurred on the Cross became more clarified, and that we were totally redeemed from Adam's fall and an Adamic sin nature at the resurrection of Jesus, the second Adam.

Once we acknowledge Jesus as our Lord, we are no longer counted as sinners before God, but considered Saints. Jesus paid for our sin debt from the beginning of our lives to the very end. We are Saints and seated in Christ with God in Heavenly places.

I had no knowledge or understanding of the Blood of Jesus, a revelation that had escaped me despite decades of regular Sunday church attendance. No recollection of ever hearing anything taught explaining the most powerful substance in the entire Universe; the only substance that could serve as sacrifice to form the Eternal Covenant that was made between God and Jesus on our behalf; its ratification made through the resurrection of Jesus Christ. This is a permanent agreement, as are all covenants God has with His people. This is real. I am stunned that pulpits are filled with pastors teaching messages of self-improvement when the message of the Finished Work of the Cross and the Blood of Jesus screams to be heard from heaven. It must grieve God to watch how His people are ignoring the rich treasury of this deep mystery of His Son. *Thank you, Father, for your grace and for your infinite mercy toward us.*

In the days ahead following my husband's confession, I was in counseling 2-3 times per week trying to process all that was happening. In April 1998, just two months after his confession, an F-4 tornado left suburban Birmingham, Alabama; bee-lined for, then barreled through my Dunwoody subdivision, leaving one person dead and total destruction in all directions. My house and its one short block were completely spared. I was homebound for a few days while the power company and tree cutters worked throughout the neighborhood restoring it to normalcy. I had joined the church that I had been attending in Dunwoody on Sunday evenings. My new pastor heard about the damage and called to check on me and my property. He had some baseline knowledge of what was happening in my marriage and understood that this was now one large problem stacked upon even greater ones. I was just one single person in a new and growing congregation and his words of concern and that simple act of knowing that someone noticed my suffering was a great source of comfort.

Most all of my friendships at this time were social relationships with friends from college, and although very dear to me, held no spiritual depth. There were practically no relationships with anyone with whom I felt I could be transparent with details of this personal magnitude. Because I had never been through anything that was so "breaking", I never fully understood the importance of having a really close knit group of authentic, Christian friends that would protect frailties and offer non-judgmental counsel and support.

This experience started me on a path of understanding the essential nature of living in community and being connected to people who could be closely trusted and to whom I could reach for in times of great need; people to cling to through life's journey and ones that enjoy the same values and goals and priorities. My closest friends to this day came from a 5 year window of time in Atlanta. Due to similarities in our circumstances, we walked, arms locked together, through a forever life bonding experience that could never be substituted with "normal" day to day living. To complicate matters, I made the decision not to tell my family what was happening because if the marriage did pull through, I felt sure it would be impossible for them to overlook the extreme nature of the circumstances. His family lived out of state as well and was basically watching to see how everything played out, and not overjoyed that he had moved out of the house. The decision to remain separated was quite sound and one that provided the maximum amount of protection for me both emotionally and physically. I have no regrets of that decision.

Unable to shoulder the full load of managing my business but unwilling to just remain at home and obsess about the problems, I contacted my new church to ask if they needed any volunteer assistance. Their request was for a data processor so I gladly accepted the volunteer position and typed in information day after day, a numbing exercise yet it kept my mind from turning over and over on all my personal issues. There were only about 10 people on staff at that time so I performed additional administrative tasks as became necessary.

In June 1998, still enjoying the lighter work load because it was enabling me to process with more clarity the heavier personal load, I was asked by an Associate Pastor if I would like to join the team as the Administrator in his department. Not anticipating this invitation, I asked for time to consider this decision because it meant closing my business and taking a cut in annual pay from $150,000 to $38,000.

At age 37, most weeks I was personally netting $600 per day, and that was after all expenses and payroll had been met. My performance-based, rational flesh struggled hard as this was not my idea of a traditional successful career move. Degreed from an admired women's college, my ambition led me down a very secular career path and I had never been taught or understood that God could truly prosper me or use my type of gifts in a ministry setting. The other wildcard was whether or not this extreme salary shift would send my finances into a death spiral. I had lots of questions.

Fortunately, very fortunately, while still emotionally shattered, God used a broken state of mind to bypass my rationale and steer me into the direction of serving Him. My normally highly analytical mind had simply shut down so I used happiness and peace as my gauge, knowing that I truly enjoyed the people with whom I was working and the tasks I was being hired to fulfill. Tired of working with clients in rigid corporate bottom-line driven business settings, a grace filled environment seemed a welcome respite for my (now very) weary soul. A change was in order and trying to take it a day at a time while not looking down the road at any potential consequences, I knew that I could no longer balance a demanding schedule filled with secular busyness while making critical decisions about my marriage and the rest of my life. The ministry doorway that swung open by God's grace was unanticipated and to the best of my ability to discern God's hand at that time, I believed that the opportunity had come from Him and not from anything that I had done, neither had I pursued it.

In hindsight, the appropriate reason to work for a church or any ministry is always that you passionately wish to bring others closer to Jesus and a higher understanding of Him; being truly called into ministry after hearing the voice of God. This was not my experience. I was at the right place at the right time with the right people maintaining the right attitude through a very deep personal crisis. There was a need on the team for someone with my skills and I got noticed. God opened a *doorway of grace* for me to enter a place that could use my gifts while allowing me a much healthier place to walk through this dark time and then begin to heal. Truthfully, I would not have recognized a "ministry call" at that time if the call was standing with a sandwich board sign on itself heralding "This is a Ministry Call!" God was speaking to me in a spiritual dimension and although it made no sense I began to walk toward the light of The Church, ignoring the fear of the unknown.

In the fall of 1998, the church offices moved into its new facility just north of Atlanta and immediately the church experienced spectacular, even vertical growth. Although hired to be an Administrator, my primary duties quickly focused on coordinating Single Adult events, church-wide conferences and facilitation of all non-production aspects of a very large college and single adult interdenominational weekly gathering. I was able to quickly use my skills and background in managing and marketing to work in this ministry setting which was extremely gratifying. The very small church staff was meeting large numbers of people, trying to simultaneously develop the church structure while shepherding the people into environments that would grow these new members spiritually and "lead people into a growing relationship with Jesus Christ". As a new believer, I was growing and learning along with everyone else we were shepherding.

In those very early days, the all-staff meetings were held in a ministry room where the pastors would address everyone, discuss internal church related topics then break up into small groups to pray over staff needs as well as the needs of people in the congregation. The very first time that I ever prayed publicly was in one of these small groups of 4-5 staff and on this particular day the Senior Pastor was in my group. I was the last person to pray and truly felt that I would black out from fear before my turn came around - my prayer probably sounded something close to reciting the Pledge of Allegiance followed up by humming a few bars of *Kumbaya* – yet finishing with a strong and confident "Amen!" This may have been the longest 2 minutes of my life but without a doubt I believed the reason the church was growing was due to my prayer prowess. My prayer life strengthened (thankfully), as I moved through the process of this transition. Prayer became a staple of my day and today I am a grateful Intercessor and one that finds the greatest joy in interceding for the church, for our nation, and for others. Prayer is the cornerstone of faith and lays the foundation for a strong and healthy relationship with the Father along with reading His Word.

PERSPECTIVE

During this season, I was definitely depending upon God to show me what to do and He did. In looking back on this remarkable yet extremely challenging season, I marvel at how God brought me to just the right people and organizations in the perfect time and season that they were needed. The only thing I can take any credit for is that I continued to press forward. God could not have brought me into the right places unless or until I was actually in motion then HE opened the right doors, then HE brought me to the right people and right church then HE put these thoughts and places on my heart.

God wants us to MOVE while yielding to His desires and listen for what He is trying to tell us. If we make a wrong turn, and we are still yielded toward Him in faith, HE can turn us around to the right place. Being in prayer is crucial because it is by prayer that we yield ourselves to Him and hear from His Spirit. Prayer is a gift from God to us and as we lift our prayer petitions to Him, He is faithful to not only listen but respond.

In my natural mind, I would have never thought to pray for a ministry position – I simply could not get my analytical mind around this one. Shifting from being a business owner over to church administration felt like a career step backward but God was not interested in my business career. He saw all that was going to happen in the future and He had moved ahead to create preparation for not only the current season but the next season. God is omniscient, omnipotent and omnipresent and has foreknowledge of all things for all people. It is important not to ignore doors that open on which you do not press ~ always pray diligently at these times to discern if this is an invitation from God for you.

Chapter Three

A Closed Door, an Opened Stain Glass Window

After six months of separation, I agreed to participate in counseling sessions with my husband with a well-respected counselor while still clinging to my other counselor on the side. Each session delved deeper and deeper into our issues as a couple and his personal issues, stirring up a great deal of anger and emotion – making me feel sick and more in pain coming out of the session than before walking into the session. Each time I left counseling with him, I was emotionally and at times even physically, shredded. My husband was meeting separately with the counselor prior to our meetings, and came under legal protection so when I tried to find out if he was telling me the truth about abstaining from his dangerous addictive behavior, the counselor could not legally release the information even though it was for my own protection. I did not realize what was happening and had been desperate for someone to defend me believing that this counselor could help as he was considered an expert in this type of behavior. We went round after round but then I finally left as it was doing more emotional damage to me than allowing Jesus to transform me from the inside out and calm my grieving heart.

At this time, I was 38 years old, married and yet for all purposes single, living with no benefits of marriage. The degree of deception and betrayal that had occurred was high and wide. I did not trust my husband, or now even our counselor, to work on my behalf to protect me or even trust that this consultative approach was in my best interest. Very green in "God knowledge", how to trust and why to trust God was still very much being revealed and the understanding of Holy Spirit was practically totally uncharted territory.

In 1999, it became essential for me to become more strongly equipped with a tangible source of power as my life became increasingly more complex due to the continued downward spiral of the marriage. Separation is a very difficult process – everything in me wanted to either remain married (which I would not do with a husband in advanced, active promiscuity) or to be divorced, which most women would have chosen immediately under these extreme circumstances. My choice to separate was based on my hope that the behavior would cease altogether. The longer I remained in marital status limbo, the harder it became on a number of levels.

These tightening circumstances opened a door to my need for and introduction to the ministry of the Holy Spirit. In 1999, my desire strengthened for a deeper connection to God and I began to learn about the Holy Spirit through watching Joyce Meyer's television programs. I taught **Battlefield of the Mind** in a small group study and read several of her books. This was the first time that I was introduced, or at least grasped the concept of spiritual warfare and that the enemy would or even could access our minds. It was also where I learned about our susceptibility in the spirit realm. It is necessary to recognize the difference between a thought that came from God and a thought, idea and suggestion that could come to us like a fiery dart from the enemy. These thoughts are always ones over which we can claim authority and take dominion. The emotions of shame, rejection, depression, confusion, and fear began to look differently. Because I learned that we are all made in the image of God, I saw that these very damaging feelings were not from Him and these emotions became "things" that were occurring outside of me and were not really a part of who I was, and that I could actually control them. Emotions were happening to me, and I did not have to allow them to happen through me, plus I had the ability to keep them from taking root.

Years later, I would come to understand that through the finished work at Calvary, the shed blood of Jesus, this ability to rightfully own peace was specifically purchased by Jesus through the blood shed from the crown of thorns worn on His head and through the bloodshed in the Garden of Gethsemane. Jesus' covenant name is Jehovah Shalom – *God our Peace* - we claim our authority over anything that comes against the peace in our minds.

This realization also started me on a journey of discerning spirits and engaging in deep intercessory prayer to help relieve the intense stress, pressure and fear that was coming against me through this complete lifestyle shift. The Holy Spirit began to train me on how to hear God's voice. I also enlisted Him to assist me in various ways to carry me emotionally down the path of what would eventually become the imminent demise of my marriage. God was saving to the very last, the revelation of the fullness of Jesus and preparing an opening for me to understand how to establish a true and sustainable relationship with Him.

Throughout this time, I was still very much depending on my church family for support. The church was developing a sophisticated small group system but because I was still married, I did not qualify for a Single Adult small group within the church nor did I feel or even wish to be single. There were several very good small groups geared toward married couples so I chose one and explained my situation to the leaders and they were very gracious. My rationale was that I would have the opportunity to watch healthy marriages first hand and see how Godly men treated their wives and vice versa by observing their interactions. I suppose you could call it research. The small group participants were very kind and helped me fit right in with their study. The men displayed strong Christian leadership ability and their mostly stay at home wives were kind, gentle, loving women in a traditional role. As a self-employed, ambitious and independent business-owning woman, single up until a few years prior, I was listening to all they had to say from another perspective, and grateful for what was being gleaned from their discussions. The men in this group checked on me frequently and made sure that I was properly cared for which meant everything during this particular season.

Throughout this entire experience, I knew that the Lord had placed very Godly men in my path to cover, protect and watch over me, more in fact than I probably will ever realize. Becoming a newly "uncovered" female was extremely unsettling and doubly so when my "coverer", and the one that was supposed to be caring for me, was instead responsible for my torment. Over time, I began to understand that God Himself was covering me and I watched Him do so over and over again, at times in miraculous and supernatural ways, which has continued into the 15 years that have followed since the ending of my marriage.

People will always disappoint, so it is crucial to have your identity firmly rooted in Jesus Christ and to understand what you own and the authority you have that is based in Jesus' sacrifice. When I first went to work for the church, my identity was rooted in where I attended school, my social friends, my family, my husband's family– anything and everything except in the right thing - who I was in Christ.

At this time in 1998, I was barely taking first steps on my "Jesus walk" even though I had attended church my entire life. Throughout the whole process of learning about the addiction and associated behaviors, then throughout the separation, it was my desire to find a solution and for him to get the necessary help to become healed and free from this bondage and torment in his mind. In my naïve state, I believed that behavior modification could successfully occur simply by refraining from encounters of promiscuity, totally misjudging the healing process necessary for him to be free of this addiction.

God continued to bring opportunities to encounter healthy modeling in relationships when another grace ordained intersection occurred in '99. A Pastor of a large North Texas Bible Church, and his gifted conference producer came to First Baptist Atlanta to deliver a seminar on *The Song of Solomon*. This Old Testament book is filled with symbolism and cultural references making it difficult to interpret. This is a book of the bible where most teachers fear to tread. This teacher and pastor, had exhaustively studied Song of Solomon in the Hebrew and in the Greek, extracting from it the beautiful story of King Solomon and what was reputed to be his first wife (he had 700). Solomon gives a thorough stage by stage account of their relationship beginning with attraction, then dating, courtship, intimacy, conflict (2 sessions), romance and commitment. The Pastor taught a line by line expository teaching through the entire book of the Song of Solomon, which is also referred to as Song of Songs. I had never heard, read or seen anything written on relationships from a biblical perspective and did not know that God even had a biblical blueprint for dating, courtship and marriage. This conference illuminated a pathway towards relational wholeness that most healthy people are hungry to grasp and understand.

Once again another piece of a life changing puzzle of restoration was hand delivered to me from God through His church. While in Atlanta, I began teaching Small Group bible studies and started by teaching the Song of Solomon curriculum and continued on for several additional years at another church after my move from Atlanta. Teaching this course gave me a sense of purpose as many people;

couples and single adults, attended to learn that God truly does have a design for relationship. Investing in others was restorative, shortening my healing time and moving me past my circumstances in ways that would never have occurred without this opportunity and curriculum. The two men behind the Song of Solomon conferences and associated curriculum will never completely know the impact that they made in the relationships of men and women during their 10 year investment until they get to heaven but it will no doubt be significant.

God stretched me in many ways, teaching a tremendous amount in this short timeframe. The single most important point I can make to anyone that is walking through a traumatic event is to keep walking through the valley and never medicate the pain. Be present to it and keep walking through it – that phrase, "When you're walking through hell, don't stop" is true! Medication can be defined as working extremely long hours, consuming numbing amounts of alcohol or drugs, or having unmarried serial sex. These are all fruitless, damaging approaches because the root of the problem never gets healed, but simply becomes numbed out and stuffed down. The mind defaults to bitterness and unforgiveness which more frequently than not impacts long term health both physical and emotional. Most every disease has a spiritual root which is directly connected to several diseases. For instance, left alone to fester, unforgiveness and bitterness are physical killers. Emotional pain is numbed, and the real issues and affiliated emotions are never fully addressed, and merely stuffed down. They will forever continue to surface if not identified and dealt with. Walking upright straight through the problems and through the pain allowed me to experience and actually feel every layer of the grief process which was crucial to my thorough healing. It felt like walking through a death.

I remained married, walking through several years in the marriage with knowledge of this addictive sexual behavior and throughout an over one year-long separation. In the middle of this separation after the shock had worn off, everything in me wanted to exit the process; get the divorce finalized quickly, find a job where I could see a visible track where I knew my salary would increase, and I had clear opportunity for advancement, and so on. I experienced days of great anger and deep sorrow coupled with protracted seasons of joy and extreme closeness to God, and then some days of feeling totally at rest.

Despite hitting every emotional high and low note on the scale, I can still affirm with confidence, that the way to walk out free, and with minimal self-condemnation and maximum peace, is to walk slowly through the pain. It is appropriate here to clarify that I do not condone divorce – my parents divorced while I was in college which set me up early for being adamantly opposed to the dissolution of any marriage. The damage incurred when my family dissolved while I was away at school had a profound impact in ways that did not completely surface until I was going through my own marital trial. Thankfully, God has healed me of that, too.

The initial approach of trying to save my marriage was

worth every minute of time taken and was done so with the highest of intentions. The death of a marriage no matter what the circumstances surrounding it, feels like a death of a person; and denial, anger, and grief are all important phases to acknowledge, accept and embrace but then release. It has been said that divorce is worse than death and I agree with that statement.

Most people try to avoid pain when a marriage is failing or beginning to fail and immediately start looking for a mate replacement or dating while they are only separated. This is the worst possible approach. If one is separated, that is not an ended marriage and in the eyes of the Church and certainly God's eyes, this constitutes an act of adultery. Re-marriages within a 2 year timeframe are the norm but with very few exceptions, are an unhealthy antidote, actually robbing the person of God's best outcome and the opportunity for full transformation. Allowing God to heal, cleanse, restore and replace broken pieces takes time yet it is time never wasted. Experiencing emotional pain should be considered normal if viewed as a means to the desired end of strengthened emotional health – peace and joy prevailing.

There are things that God wants to show and do for you in any time of extreme trial. You can miss His direction and open doors if your mind is tense, cluttered and distracted and not at some degree of rest. Minimizing stress around you, even if it means down-scaling from your current position to a less demanding one, while experiencing a difficult trial or traumatic event, is worth every lifestyle change because of what God can develop inside of you. No well managed project or big sale or high profile new client can develop in you what walking correctly through a very deep valley can do through God's guidance, partnership and Spirit-inspired direction. Character development can last a lifetime. You will never miss those big sales, or new clients, or ambition-satiating projects but your flesh will scream that you are moving in the wrong direction throughout the scale down and transition. Once you gather your courage and walk through the door that God opens to allow you to hear, heal and rest, when you have transitioned safely over and into your new position, then and only then will flesh screams subside. I can almost guarantee that this new position will not initially entail earning higher profits. If you walk out with a clean heart and a soul at rest, there is no price you can place on that "position". No higher salary, or larger home, no prestigious neighborhood or higher priced luxury automobile is even remotely comparable to strengthened, well-developed character matched with a peaceful soul and mind.

I remain grateful that during the most difficult periods of the downward spiral of my marriage, I was working in an environment that allowed me to have very "down" days and gave me the time to walk slowly through those days. The people surrounding me were highly productive, using their gifts and talents in a grace-filled, environment. Although for the most part I, too, possessed a high degree of functionality, when I needed to gear down, my supervisor kindly allowed me that liberty. The position for which God had opened a door for me was directly involved in changing the lives of others and was also a vital part of changing my own.

Throughout the process, I was authentically committed to working out the marriage and moving through the separation in a way that was not dishonoring to God. I developed friendships with single adults and enjoyed their company but shied away from anything that could appear compromising or could be morally tempting in any way. After being separated for almost a year, a friend gave me very sound advice; if the marriage did fail, I needed to adopt a two year "post-divorce" window to even begin dating again. In retrospect, this could have provided the right amount of time for restoration and to strengthen my relationship with God while allowing for a recalibration of sorts – for the re-set button to be pushed and to move forward. Truthfully, I stepped out of this timeframe because I met an extraordinary man two months following the finalization of my divorce. He lived out of state and we maintained a long distance relationship for 9 months but I was simply not emotionally ready to date and trust someone in a deep relationship, or consider re- marriage following a marital trial of this magnitude. I certainly have desired that the timing had been different.

PERSPECTIVE

There are no words that I could speak or write that could adequately express my appreciation for the church that offered me a staff position while I was walking through this deep valley that no doubt would have been much deeper without this doorway of grace opening for me. It would not be an overstatement to say that this act of favor probably saved my life. The Holy Spirit is the One that bestows favor and opens doors for God's people. Holy Spirit is released into a person that accepts Jesus as the son of God and embraces a relationship with Him. He is your closest friend and ally and is referred to, among many things, as the Comforter, the Advocate, and the Teacher. He, too, makes intercession for you to God as does Jesus. Acknowledge the Holy Spirit in your prayer time, and ask Him to be dominant in your life and to fill you from head to toe. Be bold in asking Him to grant favor in every ministry place and in every marketplace environment in which you inhabit and watch Him open doors of uncommon favor that could only come as His blessing to you.

There is the temptation to push God away during times of deep stress and anxiety. If you are finding it difficult to pray for yourself, then ask close friends to intercede on your behalf. It is my sincere belief and observation that nothing happens without the prayers of a covenant person yielding to God in prayer for another. Prayer is God's system for communication. He has a separate system for finances than the world through his protective process of tithing. He has a separate system of promotion than the world through promoting through channels of servant leadership. His systems look different but they are better. Begin your journey with prayer today and ask Him to reveal methods of prayer to you in your journey and He will do that for you. He created you for relationship so meet with Him in a quiet, specially set apart place for the purposes of communing with Him. Your life will never be the same as you learn to intercede for yourself as well as for others. Be confident yet respectful in your prayer time.

Address Him by His Covenant Hebrew names:

Jehovah Jireh	Provider	Genesis 24:14
Jevoha Ra-ah	Shepherd/Pastor	Psalm 23:1
Jehovah Rapha	Healer	Exodus 15:26
Jehovah Shalom	Peace	Judges 6:24
Jehovah Nisi	Defender/Protector	Exodus 17:15
Jehovah Shammah	His Presence	Ezekiel 48:35
Jehovah Tsidekenu	Righteousness	Jeremiah 23:6

Chapter Four

The Power of Healing Prayer

Following a year separation, in summer 1999, my husband returned back to our home after living in another friend's house. He had remained in very close communication with his sponsor and a counselor. Although I had asked him to return home in an honest attempt to restart the marriage, my trust was completely dismantled. He took a job working north of the city, returning home each night at a very late hour. Within a short timeframe, it became obvious that the addiction had not released as additional problems began to surface that were merely symptomatic of the primary root issue. Because of the repeated unwillingness and at that time inability to discontinue the addictive behavior that was dangerous to me and to him, I filed for divorce which was granted in December 1999. I was totally spent from the deception. At 34, I had innocently walked into a union with someone that had little intention or even ability at that time to be "one-d" with anyone.

He immediately moved back to his home town and I did not see him again until a brief encounter one year later when he returned to my now Atlanta home to retrieve his personal items granted in the divorce decree. My former husband's family suspended all communication; mother and father-in-law, aunts, uncles, sister- in-law, brother-in-law, etc. from the day the divorce papers were served. My father-in-law did not go into the attorney's office for the deposition and was not present for any questioning but simply showed up to retrieve his son following the deposition then drove away. This was the last time that I ever saw him.

It is my sincere belief as well as understanding, that my former husband is now healed by the grace of God from this addiction and has even counseled other men that have struggled in this same area of sexual addiction. Healing from this deep level of torment; spirits of addiction, and lust, can only be delivered by the Holy Spirit, accepting the love of God as well as understanding the meaning of the sacrifice of Jesus. Several years after returning back to his home town, he married a beautiful widow with children and they live a Christ-centered life. While attending a banquet years after the divorce, I accidentally learned of his engagement. The following day wrote a letter telling him that he had been forgiven many years prior and that I wished him great happiness in his new marriage. This was sincere and more for his benefit than for my own. To my surprise, I received an immediate letter returned to me the day that he had received my letter that was very gracious. A closed chapter and To God be the glory.

Fifteen years following the end of my marriage, I have adapted criterion for courtship but it could only happen because of the strengthening of my relationship with the Holy Spirit. Physical attraction or being attracted to the way a person looks is perfectly natural and very important but the single most important marker of a person's ability to be the right one for another Christian is by promptings from the Holy Spirit and anything less is merely a good guess. The Holy Spirit, your internal GPS given to you as a gift from Jesus, will let you know if someone is to be your mate and

His information will probably come when you are not looking. He will coordinate your steps and intersect the two of you when you expect it least or open your eyes to see a person in a new and different way with whom you have known for years.

> *Who has directed the Spirit of the Lord or as His counselor has taught Him? With whom did He take counsel, that instruction might be given Him? Who taught Him the path of justice and taught Him knowledge and showed Him the way of understanding?* -Isaiah 40:13-14

Still employed by the church following the divorce, I remained focused on my responsibilities. One day in 1999, standing alone in the church auditorium preparing for the evening's service, I saw myself teaching to hundreds and hundreds of people. No one was in there – this was like a vision that I saw in the Spirit. This actually happened twice within one year.

During this same time frame, the Lord began to give me a burden to return back to Alabama, specifically my home town of Tuscaloosa, a college town and community with a population of 120,000. I had never desired to return home so knew that this burden was from the Lord as it was definitely not coming from within me. The desire to return back to Alabama became stronger and stronger yet was confusing because I had little relationship with my family or anyone that lived in that city. Sadly, for many years, I was strictly a holiday guest and we were little more than related strangers. My parent's had divorced while I was away at college, yet both had remarried; my father to a wife with two young children and my mother married a man with four "out of the nest" adult children. My brother remained in our hometown following his graduation from University of Alabama and had made a life there while maintaining relationships with our parents despite the re-marriages. In short, I could not figure out how or why the Lord wanted me to return to Alabama. I had never wanted to return and it made absolutely no sense in the natural but this was a burden that was with me day and night.

Concurrently, remaining on this church staff was becoming more difficult as my new singleness had single home ownership responsibilities attached and my church salary was now not balancing with my expenses. The combined desire to leave Atlanta, plus the financial difficulty of remaining in the house was draining and regrettably I allowed the stress and fear to get the better of me.

The house went on the market and I waited for it to sell then waited and waited some more. The house was not getting shown, and because of my great desire to move away and to start a new chapter, my discouragement slid into a deep anger-based depression. A handy non-clinical definition for depression is *anger turned inward* and I had plenty of that working.

I found an interim job with a friend's company that was paying me a higher salary than what I had been making. Although I had owned a successful marketing and staffing company prior to working in the ministry, there was enough of a time lapse to make it impossible to resurrect my company. Employers were reluctant to hire someone that had been employed in a ministry setting into a marketplace management position. Unfortunately, the business world has little understanding of the ministry world but ministry-minded people are quite an asset to any company.

During this difficult period of transition back into secular business, a recommendation came to take a 28 week spiritually based program that offered a very deep healing experience by my now former God- sent counselor. I prayed about this and felt the Lord's direction to take the house off the market, which would leave me enough time to take the course uninterrupted by the distraction of a return move back to Alabama. This course was my first exposure to deep healing prayer. The class structure was that each week a speaker addressed a specific area of brokenness then we were dismissed to our small groups for our leaders to pray healing prayers over us relating to our individual circumstances. No one but our group leaders spoke during this time – we were asked to simply receive these individualized prayers. My poor group leader had more than her share of ground to cover with me. Layers of pain had accumulated over the course of my entire lifetime and were now painfully peeling off like an old onion skin – layers that had clouded my perception in relationships, layers that had unknowingly masked deep pain from my childhood where I was carrying anger and emotional scars. A large layer had never been dealt with surrounding my early childhood as well as my parent's divorce and the collapse of my family.

I am convinced that the primary reasons that I am healed

from the deep wound of betrayal of my marriage today is from these prayers of healing, my intentionality in working this course and finally, forgiving my former husband and others. Had I ignored the quiet prompting from the Lord to take this course, my re-entry back to Alabama would have resembled something more like a spaceship returning into the earth's atmosphere; jerking and shaking from G- force rather than what it became; smooth, grounded and forward-focused. It fascinates me at times to look back over the vantage point of several years and see how God's hand was at work in my life. Recently, I have been praying for God not to let me miss the "Big Rocks", those large rocks in a stream that you step on that really get you to the other side. It's those big rocks that are the anchors and even if you sidetrack on the smaller ones – the big ones always need to rise up and come into focus in their correct time and season. *Father, please don't ever let us miss those big rocks.*

Three days after completing the seminar, I placed a For Sale by Owner sign in my yard and 2 days later a divinely timed young couple drove by the house then called my number for an appointment. Voila! Within 3 days, they put a contract on the house and it sold, releasing me out from under its financial obligation. This confirmed what I suspected; that the Lord had held back the sale of my home so that I would find and take this important program on healing. The sale was somewhat bittersweet because I loved my home but it was time to move on and away from the memories it held by no fault of its own. My wonderful church small group members came over and assisted me in packing up the house for the movers to take my furniture on to Alabama.

When I made the original decision to leave my church staff position, my supervising pastor was given an advance notice of one full year. I honestly did not believe it would take a full year to find and prepare a replacement but understood that my position was more complex than anyone understood and would be difficult to replace. In the end, my position was broken apart and my responsibilities were filled by 3 capable people.

Because the house sold sooner than expected, I made a temporary move north to Alpharetta with minimal possessions and lived with my now best friend in her beautiful home for 6 months while making the necessary arrangements to return to Alabama. Remaining in Alpharetta following my home sale was to allow me time to determine whether to move to Birmingham or move back home 60 minutes further south. This was time well spent because I was still healing, I had become too isolated in my own home and this interim step gave me even further opportunity to get where I needed to be before wading out into the water of departing from everything and everyone that I had known for 13 years.

My pattern in decision-making had changed from my college years and in my 20's from being very spontaneous with little planning or consideration for detail to one now at 40 which was much more methodical, trying to be keenly attuned to God's timing and correct seasons. In truth, the jump from Atlanta down to basically an unfamiliar, small college town was more of an adjustment than I wanted to tackle, particularly after going through the emotional upheaval of a marital status change. I chose Birmingham and moved there in the spring of 2002.

Starting over at the age of 40, I was scared yet excited now having a clean canvas on which to paint my newly single-ized life. I left Atlanta with the sale proceeds from my home and was furnished with start-up capital for a consulting business based on my previous career of business ownership. I still had struggled greatly with the decision of whether to seek out a ministry position or return to a marketplace vocation. My heart was tied to ministry work but my skill set and financial needs were pointing more toward a return to the marketplace. My level of faith, although ratcheting up, was still not as high as it could have been during this transition. I had witnessed God's hand move on my behalf, and the healing class had become an essential part of my healing journey but it was still disconcerting to move to uncharted territory.

Before leaving Atlanta, I attended a highly valuable three month career assessment program initiated by a leadership development company, counseled by its co-founder. Their program helped me to pinpoint my skills, gifts, talents and values and validated the direction that was believed best for my next career move. After my repeated references to ministry work and hearing their repeated response back to me, "Your Life is Your Ministry" I finally decided to return back to the business world. In reality, ministry doors must "swing" by grace, they cannot be shoved open or forced down – God's process does not work that way. The Lord will allow these doors to open (or He will not) and only in His timing will this occur.

PERSPECTIVE

I am fascinated at how the Holy Spirit will put things on a heart, giving a burden for a city or person and then in the correct time and season, move that person towards those areas. It is as if He gives us a hint of the future, pulling back a curtain for a brief moment for a glimpse then dropping the curtain so that it will hang straight again but you have to figure out the process of getting there. God will take you down a pathway that grows and stretches, transforming you more into the likeness of Christ as you move through the experience. I believe that God gives us these experiences so that we can share them with others to carry them through similar circumstances. We are to help each other, pull each other up and God will open those doors for those purposes.

When you share your circumstances, make sure that you take the time to pray for healing with the individual with whom you are ministering – a person on the other side has the advantage to pray more specifically for another, calling on the Holy Spirit and Jesus to intercede to the Father as well as to identify and command particular influences of negative spirits to release the individual in the name of Jesus'.

When praying for healing surrounding a death or divorce; pray to ask the Holy Spirit to bind and break the spirit of Trauma, always number one, second would be to pray against Fear and Condemnation.

Chapter Five
A Supernatural Season

Moving to a new city is disconcerting and disorienting whether you know people or not but I knew no one for all purposes. It was my highest priority, after finding a place to live, to connect into a new church family as quickly as possible but also knowing that I needed to hear from God to make the right choice. The process for most people will begin the same way and will end the same way; you visit church after church until you hopefully hear the Holy Spirit say…THIS IS YOUR HOME! This is exactly what I did. Because of my close connection to my previous church home, I was convinced that God lived directly only over North Atlanta but did, however consider that He might make intermittent field trips to fly over Birmingham and other cities. I went about my search unconvinced that I would find what I was seeking in a community of believers.

In looking back at the shift in my theology from 1998 to 2002, there was a significant movement in my spiritual walk and theology at the end of those 3 years. Through the tragedy of the loss of my marriage, the change in my career and the financial peaks and valleys, walking forward and seeking a relationship with God and other Christian people grew and stretched me in ways that I could have never experienced had I not accepted God's invitation to walk through an earlier door of ministry.

As I began looking for a Birmingham church, I was more

receptive to theologies involving the Holy Spirit because my life had required much more than just living in a "natural state" to survive. The stress, anger, rejection, fear and constant perceived uncertainty of my previous situation had pushed me emotionally to a place where, at times, I had not wanted to continue living. This became a much stronger consideration after leaving my job at the church, primarily due to isolation, as my depression became deep and sustained. The attempts to sell my house were not working; finances were low, my church family was gone, and I could not move forward and get out of Atlanta. Everything about my life had felt "locked up" yet I was sure that the Lord had also been preparing me for a move away from Atlanta. I had been emotionally pressed to the wall and it was forcing the "oil" from me – the oil of the Spirit, the greatest gift of this entire experience.

When I was able to begin moving forward in starting over again in Birmingham, I knew no one, and had no church, and no business contacts with which to launch a new career, but God continued to help me make connections (again because I continued to take steps forward) and take me down spiritual trails and by-ways that quickened and matured my walk with Him. My journey with meeting the person of Jesus, a distinct and separate experience than meeting God, had really only just begun.

In 2002, one Wednesday evening, I walked into a large suite in a small office complex adjacent to a Shelby County Wal-Mart and a skating rink. Although a 40 minute traffic-laden drive from my home, I had heard a very good report from a stranger in a retail store regarding a new start up church with a pastor that had moved to Alabama from a neighboring state. I know it was God that maintained and fueled my interest to actually drive all the way out to that location. The church was meeting on Sunday mornings in a High School auditorium – a vast difference from the 2700 seat auditorium and church complex that I had just left in Atlanta. There was something in that Wednesday night room that was undeniably powerful. I lacked the necessary discernment and full understanding of the workings of the Holy Spirit then but clearly understood that the message coming from within that 400 seat office complex auditorium was great teaching - it was different. The church was process oriented and asked the attenders to go through a 4 step "Growth Track" model that would introduce them to its doctrinal values. It then proceeded into deeper areas of revealing spiritual gifts, directing people into places of service that would fuel their passion while putting them closer to reaching their purpose and God's destiny for their lives.

The pastor was a textbook Transformational Leader with a natural gift of communication and discernment about what made people passionate about serving. Events that were small, intimate and energizing were offered for everyone's participation. Really for the first time, I was participating in a weekly corporate prayer environment with resources and materials that were helping me grow and develop as an Intercessor for the church and for others. My prayers on how to learn to pray effectively while on staff in Atlanta were now being answered within this Body. He began to open my mind to the subject of physical healing as well.

Over a 7 year period, I had several significant supernatural occurrences with the one common denominator of prayer during this long season in Birmingham; most notably 3 miracle physical healings in my body. One can unwaveringly believe that God is still very much in the healing business.

In 2002, I flew to Russia with my best friend from college to have her initial meeting with 3 year old twins that she was adopting from an orphanage in Tyumen, Siberia. Although she had arranged for us to stay in very fine accommodations throughout the trip and we tried to be conscientious about everything consumed, the food was unfamiliar and apparently I made a highly detrimental lapse in food judgment. By the grace of God, the illness I contracted while over there did not strike until the night I returned from the trip back to the states - my symptoms became near violent, almost requiring hospitalization from the dehydration. This mystery illness, which started in my gut, eventually somehow traveled and settled in my right ear causing loud tinnitus, vertigo and severe headaches. I sought treatment from an ENT who was very unnerved by what he was seeing because the condition could easily cause severe hearing loss. I had been totally deaf in my left ear since age 5 from the Mumps, contracted due to an ineffective MMP vaccine taken in childhood. For 5 years, I continued to suffer near debilitating sessions of headaches and vertigo from whatever I had picked up in Russia.

One Sunday afternoon in the summer of 2007, I was experiencing an extreme case of headaches and dizziness, causing me to be sofa-bound, and to miss church. Strong emotion rose up within me. Angry, I simply decided that I was not going to accept that pain another minute. I had been reading *Blessings and Curses* by Derek Prince, and in it there is a prayer for the release of a curse. By this point, I was feeling pretty cursed so I sat up, and read that long prayer aloud then told God that I just would not accept this pain and vertigo anymore. Swinging my legs around, I lay back down on my side on the sofa. Within an instant, my inner right ear experienced the hand of God moving within it. I felt His hand move in my inner ear and slowly turn, correcting the problem, while parts of my ear were popping and literally moving! My ear had been miraculously recalibrated back to its original design and functioning power. I could hardly believe what had just happened. There was no pain involved in the experience, just a supernatural hand re-setting of my inner ear. The vertigo and headaches were gone immediately. You can believe that this brought the phrase "the miracle working hand of God" new meaning up close and very personal. I have only told this story a few times and mostly in intimate church small group settings because it sounds so incredulous but still today, I remain free and clear of this condition.

My second healing occurrence involved my C4 and C5 neck discs. Upon being clinically diagnosed with degenerative disc disease which has run in my mother's family for at least two generations; I would have made the third generation had the devil's scheme not been stopped through an alert intercessor. I was seeing a chiropractor routinely in Atlanta and then again in Birmingham for adjustments and relief from pain around these constantly inflamed and swollen discs and had even started traction in his office to relieve the pressure off them. A couple from my church was hosting a healing small group and as an avid student of healing since 1990, I jumped in with great anticipation. Each week we listened to a teaching on healing then prayed for individuals in the group. There were numerous emotional and physical health needs among them or group members would stand in for friends and family that needed physical or even emotional healing.

In one session, one young lady was being prayed for by several people and one of the older ladies turned around in mid-sentence prayer, grabbed the back of my neck and started praying something aloud in her prayer language. Startled, I did not quite know what to think – she did not know anything about this disc issue, but I let her keep going because I had been in tremendous pain and believed that God was working though her. I had been sitting on the floor, stood up and felt the same way that I had entered the session the remainder of the evening. The next morning, when I awoke there was absolutely no pain in those discs and I had increased flexibility. God had used my small group friend Mary to be a conduit for a healing miracle for one of His children. To this day, these discs are blessed and disease free – to God Be the Glory. While women on my mother's side of the family are still struggling with disk and neck problems, I believe that the generational spirit was broken in me, thus breaking the line.

Another prominent healing miracle came when God

delivered me from a long-standing deep and at times debilitating pain in my right hip. Again, my maternal family line almost all struggle with hip issues– primarily arthritis. For years I had experienced pain in the right hip joint, at times even making it difficult to walk comfortably and exercise was even cumbersome. Once again, I reached a breaking point and determined with my will not to tolerate this condition. I began to pray prayers of healing aloud daily, praying specifically for my bones, joints, and muscles to align with God's perfect will for them which are always complete health and wholeness. One day I began to notice that my hip was simply no longer hurting – I was able to walk and run for distances without having to stop due to discomfort. My hip had come into complete alignment and agreement with the will and the word of God on its very own through my body hearing my own words of healing being spoken aloud through prayer.

PERSPECTIVE

These are just a few of the miracle healings that God has performed in my body. These illustrations were chosen because the original conditions were all medically documented. I have numerous other brief illnesses and infirmities that have been "blessed out" by God through my own prayers and the prayers of others. Most of my own healings have occurred through my personal prayer time as I have gained more confidence and have learned how to take authority over illnesses and emotions and how to enlist the Holy Spirit, asking Him to apprehend any spirit in my body that is not of God. Our right to complete freedom and healing has been fully purchased at the Cross through the perfect

Son's sinless blood. We need only walk in the authority of the name of Jesus and the blood of Jesus.

It is the Holy Spirit that knit each one of us in the womb of our mother's and so He knows everything about how we are made because He crafted us Himself! I call on Him frequently and we have developed a close relationship, honoring Him daily and acknowledging His presence and power in my life. It is the Spirit that goes in and does a miracle healing for someone – He is the verb and action of the Trinity – a great mystery of the Deity. Healing occurs by and through the stripes of Jesus; His sacrifice that purchased us and that ratified our eternal covenant with God. Jesus now remains seated and resting at the right of hand of the Father, interceding for us day and night. I think we can all agree that He has done enough and in fact His work is Finished just as He proclaimed Himself from the cross. It is the Spirit whose power is released to others for healing and it is the Spirit within that allows you to self-heal and self-deliver. That's right – you can heal and deliver yourself and I have done so more times than I could even count by calling on the power of the Holy Spirit while demanding that my soul and body submit to the Spirit and God's will for complete health and wholeness.

It is because of Jesus' blood and the purchased benefit from Jehovah Rapha, Our Healer, that we can now walk in divine health that we now not only own our healing but we must fix our minds in confidence that by His stripes we are healed. We need not fight from a defeated stance, but we now stand victorious – from a healed position already won. My own personal experiences with healing, understanding of the finished work and the power of Christ's blood have culminated in an unwavering belief that it is never the will of our heavenly Father for His children to walk in sickness and disease.

Chapter Six

Good is the Enemy of Best

During my 8.5 year season in Birmingham, I took a freedom and deliverance-lite course taught within my home church, attending classes as a participant, and over time, integrating into its leadership structure as a small group leader and an Intercessor serving with them for several years. The course concentrated on emotional healing; freeing people from past hurt and regrets, as well as dealing with behavior modification; i.e. watching your words, maintaining your body as a clean vessel to be a greater conduit for God's power. All of which is important information, particularly for people that are new to the body of Christ however the motivation behind the actions should come due to an increased knowledge and love of Christ, a genuine desire to be more like Him and an understanding that deliverance is provided through a gift of grace accomplished through the finished work of Jesus and a focus on God's immutable love. Holiness striving is counterfeit good to God's best.

After several years of being actively involved with the retreats and classes, myself and others were seeing a noticeable level of spiritual attacks coming onto the leaders. An influential leader in this ministry division was primarily responsible for fueling what ensued following a one on one, confidential comment that I made regarding these attacks. My comment of concern was made to one church associate who in turn leveraged the information for an agenda.

Fortunately, and over time, I have come to view this breaking away from this man-made deliverance ministry as an essential part of my journey towards a greater and deeper revelation of healing, intercessory prayer and grace. This breaking allowed God to impart a spiritual truth to me regarding the finished work and the freedom that has been purchased for everyone that calls on the name of Jesus. When the Spirit administers healing through the framework of the acknowledgement of the atoning work of Jesus, there are no demonic attacks. Furthermore, we are already made free, having been delivered by His sacrifice, an essential truth that we must embrace. You already have it. We stand and pray from a posture of victory, not p l e a d i n g from defeat. All deliverance actions must flow only through the body and blood of Jesus Christ and the acceptance of His work as being complete. All else is less than; maybe good, and with some success, but certainly not God's highest, or best. Other freedom models are man-engineered, prone to personal agendas, egos and "religion". It is only Jesus that heals – not any man or any woman.

In the summer of 2007, I joined a launch team that was starting a campus plant from the main church. I drove back and forth each Sunday, in part, to put distance between me and the self-professed and religious freedom experts but also to bring this Spirit filled, and what I believed to be highly relevant, pastor's teaching to my home town. As I continued my involvement with the new church plant, I felt the Lord open my eyes to more possibility in that city as well as bringing to remembrance again the burden that He had placed on me for it while working for the

Atlanta church.

In early July 2009, I met with the Senior Pastor of the church and discussed my desire to move, explaining that I had heard from the Lord that one day I would return and believed that the timing for me was at that point. While presenting this explanation, I pulled out a framed photograph of the Atlanta church's auditorium filled with people and immediately felt a confirmation from the Holy Spirit that this was a Kairos moment, or God's appointed time to act as the Holy Spirit draws near to do a special work. In short, I believed He was showing me I was moving in the right direction because oftentimes it is so hard to know. Ten years prior in Atlanta, the Lord had prepared me for a 2 year period for my return back to Alabama following my 23 year hiatus. Some of this preparation manifested in a supernatural way. I felt a similar unsettling and readiness stirring inside me for some length of time around this move as well.

Unfortunately the church launch experience was awkward, having multiple leadership challenges on a staff and volunteer level. At that time, this church would simply not take root in the city but me and 3-4 people from the main church continued to travel south an hour each Sunday for 2.5 years. I put my home on the market 10 days after meeting with the Senior Pastor and started the process of looking for a job and networking to get back home. My objective in Tuscaloosa was to work in a full time ministry capacity, and one that embraced a Holy Spirit-filled theology. There had been no conversation with my current church affiliation regarding a position but I was hopeful to find a para-church ministry that was a good fit. The high degree of unknowns with my return were met with terror filled levels of reservation and a lack of trust that anything about this could turn out favorably. This does not sound very spiritual, but at that time, this was the truth. I was over-analyzing everything about the decision and almost losing my mind in the process.

Because of my training and high degree of interest in prayer plus what I knew to be deliverance ministry during this season, my greatest desire was to develop an intercessory prayer and healing ministry. I had located a retreat house in nearby Northport where I could get that started but needed a job as well. I was walking through this entire experience to the best of my natural ability but God had a much better plan to teach me essential disciplines in His own way without the influence of any other ministry organization and totally by His own Spirit.

Weeks turned into months in selling my Birmingham home. I was determined to make this move and become all that I believed God wanted me to be for Him. Time is the enemy of faith and will test resolve in every direction and mine was tested in ways that I did not even realize were ever possible. Much of the reticence about returning to Tuscaloosa was based in difficult memories held from my childhood as I dealt with rejection from people in my environment in my formative years. Never connecting with the town as a child or youth, I was one that always required more mental stimulation than most of my young peers, dreaming vastly different dreams for myself. Not the least bit interested in sports, and bored in a community sports-rich culture, I always wanted to live in a larger, innovative city with all of their cultural and marketplace offerings so a return back to a small college town with no job or place to live was causing much confusion. If God wants you to do something and puts you on an assignment, shouldn't it be easy? I quickly learned that life could become even more difficult and complex trying to live out His desires.

To submit fully to the task ahead, in September 2009, I gave myself an unusual birthday / pre-return home gift by signing up to meet with a deliverance team that had worked and traveled with Derek and Ruth Prince. Prior to the appointment, I was mailed a lengthy packet of questions and material that was to be filled out and returned to them in advance of my 4 day session. The questions required me to go back several generations and document family member names, ages of death, reasons for death, and any known destructive habits on both sides of my family; smoking, alcohol or drug abuse, physical and emotional abuse. Through my meetings with the counseling team, I learned the names of many spirits, naming and praying through them to be bound, broken and released from generational blood lines. In 3 days in that room – 3 days even barely devoted to each reason that I was meeting with them, tormenting spirits were routed out and broken by the Holy Spirit. I question why people still associate themselves with their behaviors if they are truly free. Once someone is delivered of a spirit of addiction, or fear, or anything else there is little need for behavior modification because the tormenter is gone and the person becomes free from the desire. This is how Jesus healed as documented in the Gospels. From this point, there is no reason for a person to refer to themselves ever again as a recovering smoker, alcoholic, sex addict. The abuser has left and the mind freed. All addictions begin and are sustained from within the mind.

But this was not an all good experience. There was a 30 day "curing" period for this style of deep deliverance to actually take effect so I was sent on my way with a packet of information which included prayers, scripture verses and other instructions. Only the couple that allowed me to stay in their vacation home knew I was down there. Because of the timing of this experience, putting my home on the market and all of the distractions that are associated with moving, I apparently miscalculated the need for adhering to all of the necessary steps to proactively guard myself from these spirits returning against me, a miscalculation that almost cost me my life. Starting in October 2009, I went into a dramatic and sharp downward spiral culminating in a 6 week literal fight for my life both physically and mentally. These circumstances started very suddenly with no warning and with no obvious or evident "backsliding" from the deliverance sessions.

A primary problem for which I had sought out these practitioners was to focus on ridding me of the spirit of FEAR. I had struggled with fear as long as I could remember and was terrified to return to Tuscaloosa. The spirit of fear came back against me with a near fatal vengeance. For 6 consecutive weeks, I slept no more than 4 hours each night. My heart raced almost right out of my chest night and day. My reticence in moving to Tuscaloosa was now taking a very backseat to this problem of cataclysmic fear – this was something demonic with a mind of its own that had taken up residence within my body. My heart was being strained to its fullest capacity – feeling near heart attack level all day and every night. Before getting into bed, I would get down on my knees every night, and beg the Holy Spirit to take this vicious attack off of me. I could not get this blowtorch of fear to release. I called the deliverance practitioners and explained what was happening and pleaded with them to pray to get this to release. I spent most of my days praying to God to get this "thing" off of me before it killed me. I was experiencing chest pain, exhaustion and an abnormally rapid heart rate that would not subside. I used every bit of prayer training I knew at that time to stop this spirit plus called the deliverance team twice to enroll their help and then one day, 6 weeks later, as suddenly as it started – it stopped. I felt it lift off, just completely quit, still remembering where I was standing in my home when it departed. I knew immediately I was free.

It took many months before the confusion, anxiety and fatigue cleared from this attack, and well after my move to Tuscaloosa however, the extreme fear, rapid heart rate and insomnia ceased immediately. Lingering symptoms like fatigue, confusion, nervousness and emotional swings abounded. I was having difficulty in processing information or really doing much of anything except hope that I would survive whatever had just happened to my mind and body. My mind became a soupy confusion – struggling to process even basic information. It felt like what a nervous breakdown must feel like and probably even looked like but

I was not a nervous breakdown kind of person nevertheless, I went down, way down, but never did break. Praise God. Following this fight my mind remained in this "soupy state", dark, murky depression, and an inability to think or process anything for many months thereafter. Following this experience, I have read articles written from other ministry people that have experienced this identical attack.

I did not seek medical attention because I knew that it was spiritual and doctors would not have the proper diagnosis or protocol to treat a demonic attack, this was not science or biological in nature. Any doctor hearing my story would have believed that I was having a breakdown and try to give me drugs but I knew differently, knowing well the capacity of my own mind and body. The final evidence of this was the immediacy in which the activity started and the immediacy in which "it" vanished. The Lord taught me something very important through this terrifying experience – the Holy Spirit holds the power to wield the sword that protects our minds from spiritual attack. For 6 weeks, it felt as if the Holy Spirit fully lifted His protection off from my mind while I was mercilessly attacked by the demonic. I have re-read notes of desperation written to myself during this time that were chilling. A demonic spirit was nearly successful in killing me before I moved to Tuscaloosa. I know that the devil does not have full knowledge of the future because if he did have that ability, he would never have worked through people to facilitate Jesus' crucifixion. Of course, following the crucifixion, Jesus went down to hell and defeated the devil, making a public spectacle of demonic powers and principalities. Colossians 2:15. He must however have some useful strategic knowledge and know something about the assignment that God has planned for any of us.

The nine months prior to moving from Birmingham then the 14 months following the move were a constant stream of the most difficult, painful trials on every level of my life. It was an all-out assault on my emotions and my mind. I learned how to survive under extreme conditions, living with no certainty or security and in severe rejection in every direction, being forced to learn to trust God day to day. This experience also showed me in innumerable ways that absolutely everything comes from God's hand – period, no exceptions.

Through this invaluable experience, I earned a PhD from Fear University and conclude that an extreme and protracted state of fear is the most dangerous emotion that can impact the human mind and body. Fear acts as an open portal into a person's soul where every negative, destructive emotion and demonic spirit flows in from hell. If left unchecked or unbound, this portal of fear will release into a person's mind, all manner of destructive emotion-charged spirits; paranoia, confusion, depression, suicidal thoughts, mistrust of people in every environment. Fear is THE spirit of the devil and, in my opinion he actually lives and operates always conveniently cloaked in the emotion of fear. Fear is his dwelling place. Fear is his heaven. If a person resists fear then the enemy has nothing on which to "latch" and to impregnate a person with evil, insecurities, or just plain wrong thinking. Fear gives legal right to the demonic into a person's soul.

I was allowed to fully understand the protection that the Spirit gives us from the outer darkness as God enabled me to experience this for my benefit and for the benefit of others. I will never forget this important teaching from The Teacher about Himself. I have gained irreplaceable insight and supernatural discernment regarding mind spirits and emotions by walking through this first hand. There is a reason why there are 365 biblical references that admonish us not to fear; one for each day of the year. You must be diligent about protecting your mind from fear. Have scripture verses at the ready that declare the love of God for you and speak them aloud. The understanding of the depth and height of God's love and desire to work on your behalf birth's confidence and faith that dispels fear. God is not the one that condemns; that is the voice of the enemy. We are all perfected through love.

> *There is no fear in love. But perfect love drives out fear, because fear has to do with punishment. The one who fears is not made perfect in love.* -1 John 4:18

> *For God did not give us a spirit of timidity, (of cowardice, of craven and cringing and fawning fear), but (He has given us a spirit) of power and of love and of calm and well-balanced mind and discipline and self-control.*
> -2 Timothy 1:7 AMP

During this season I learned the most about my best friend, Holy Spirit who continues to be the unsung hero of the Holy

Trinity. The Holy Spirit's power is what resurrected Jesus to life out of that tomb. He conceived Jesus in the womb of Mary because there was no sin in Him – the sin flowing from the Adamic nature through His God- ordained father; Joseph. Jesus' bloodline came from the bloodline of God Himself, royal blood, and no man. Biologically, blood does not come from the egg of a woman and does not begin production until the egg is fertilized by the sperm and the child's body begins conception. The bloodline of a child traces paternally, the mother's role is to feed the child and nurture it in her body through the placenta; her blood does not enter her baby. There could be no egg donor for Jesus because it would have come from a tainted line of sin which is why the Holy Spirit conceived the child supernaturally in Mary's womb. The ovum that was Jesus self-produced its own blood. Jesus' bloodline is the blood of Deity belonging to God Himself and is the single most powerful substance provided for us on this earth. Where else could blood and the life of Jesus come from? Why else through its holiness and purity could it be still useful to us and powerful when applied by faith, 2000 years later, as if it was shed just yesterday?

PERSPECTIVE

Declaring the blood of Jesus over a situation initiates angelic enforcement. Angels run to respond to this just as they respond to act on God's word spoken aloud over a situation. You may hear the term "pleading the blood", like in the case of a jury pleading a case - but the case for the blood of Jesus has already been won for every Believer and is readily available to you for your personal application. No need to plead. A generous dose of faith combined with the knowledge of God's endless love and grace (undeserved, unmerited favor) for you will render the best possible result over present circumstances.

Jesus has already paid the forever price for you to be forgiven - you cannot earn your forgiveness. You are completely sanctified by His blood – sanctification is not ongoing, you are sanctified once and for all when you accept Christ as your Savior. The work of Jesus is finished and complete. Jesus is seated and resting alongside God His Father interceding (praying) for you day and night. The Holy Spirit and the blood of Jesus work together and in perfect harmony and in fact, it is my opinion that they may be inseparable. There is Spirit LIVING in the blood. Holy Spirit moves with and because of the blood and when the request is anchored in unwavering faith, He will move in ways that will astound you. We know that life is in the blood and the life of Jesus continues to reside permanently and actively in His blood for us still today.

Chapter Seven

God's Timing is Never Late

It took 10 months for my home to sell in Birmingham. Ten months of pure hell. Throughout this period of walking out God's call for me to return home, I had not found a job in either city so had practically no finances, could have barely worked if I had found a job as I was either in or recovering from this attack. There were few friends left as many had been from the group of self-professed freedom experts that were now angry despite the fact that I had tried to help them. Other friends had simply thrown up their hands, not knowing what to do with my situation. Admittedly, it did not look good. What could have been construed by some as a pure lack of initiative was in fact something much deeper and more dangerous. Add to this, the confusion created by living between two cities, unable to move forward from one to the other was also exponentially compounding the problem.

The longer I remained unable to move forward from Birmingham, the angrier I became about being "called back" to Tuscaloosa, still having no idea why God would have me return while doors in every direction were slamming shut around me where I was living. Absolutely nothing would open in that city. In Tuscaloosa, I had depended on specific friends to network and help me secure a position yet unfortunately during the time of my greatest need I was mercilessly slandered, derailing much needed opportunities for provision. Condemnation, rejection and fear were coming at me from all sides – three of the very things that I had worked so hard to deflect through the deliverance session prior to my move. Birmingham was clearly not where I was to live but I felt like a lima bean being blown through a drinking straw trying to return home. Multiple times while in Birmingham and throughout the first 14 months of living in Tuscaloosa, I was almost certain that I would not survive the transition. Fear almost killed me physically and mentally and if that had not, I considered doing it to myself as the tunnel continued to go deeper and get darker.

Through this time there were a few points of light and several unmistakable grace gifts offered by God to me during this season. My home finally sold in April of 2010, during a period when the market had bottomed out. I had purchased my home in 2006 at the top of the market but because the owner had been transferred and needed to sell, I purchased it far below its market value. My house finally sold in 2010 for almost full price to a family that ironically had donated the original office space to my Birmingham church to get them started. The daughter that bought my home was also an Intercessor and I assured her that no other house in that city had had more prayer flowing through it than mine! I also owned an investment condominium that was in an eclectic part of Birmingham called Southside. This unit had been put on the market 3 separate times over a 4 year period and had never received an offer despite the diligent work of competent Realtors. At the time I was moving to Tuscaloosa, this albatross condominium had no tenant and I was also paying all utilities, HOA fees and making the mortgage payments. My father told me that I could not move to Tuscaloosa if my condominium was vacant so my options were to rent, sell or live in it. "OK, deal," I responded.

The Thursday before the Saturday of my scheduled move down to Tuscaloosa, I received a phone call from a young woman that was looking for a place to live that fit the description of my condo. Bear in mind, I had not had a tenant in months, so the place was vacant.

She liked it and wanted her boyfriend to come back and take a look. I explained to her that I was about to move into this unit so if she liked it she needed to step on the gas and that my movers were scheduled to be at my house on Saturday morning to take my furniture on to Tuscaloosa. The boyfriend approved, she wanted it and informed me that she had no credit and needed to write a check for one full year of rental payments in advance. Nobody does that. My finances were totally drained. I was only receiving a few thousand dollars at closing, yet very grateful that I was not upside down on the mortgage. Because of the financial uncertainty, I was unsure exactly where I was going to live in Tuscaloosa and had been unsuccessful in finding a job in the small college town. The Lord was instructing me to move home so I was going. The full year of rental payments from my condominium was gratefully received as provision and confirmation from God that I was moving in the right direction. As I heard TBN's founder the late Paul Crouch, Sr. say one hundred times, "God is never early, or never late, He is always right on time."

Placing phone calls for Tuscaloosa housing, I found a place up near the lake on the end of the cul-de-sac. If I had been able to choose any place in town, this was exactly where I wanted to live and would even have had an end unit overlooking the golf course. It appeared on the surface that it was being delivered from God as a gift of obedience and for making the difficult move but while praying I could not receive an "all clear" signal. The conversations with the realty company went back and forth and we got very close to what the owner wanted but I had no contract on the unit. The day before the move, I left a message for the property manager that I was taking the unit and would be down the following day to sign the paperwork. Because it had been available all week long, I assumed that it could still be mine. The truck arrived at my house with inadequate staff to pack and move all of the furniture – it took 10 hours to move an almost already completely packed 2600 SF house 60 miles. I had been calling the Property Manager all day the day prior to take this house so as to move straight in and avoid the extreme inconvenience of moving my furniture into storage. She knew I wanted the unit.

The morning of the move, I was informed that I would not get the unit, and everything I owned had to be off loaded into a storage facility. I had no definite place to live and was emotionally working off my very last firing synapse. At the very edge, following the all-day move, I drove to my mother's house and laid down on a chaise on her back patio, shaking uncontrollably from exhaustion and the terror of just not knowing where I would live or how I would sustain myself in a city of 98% strangers. Unlike the move from

Atlanta, there had been no offer of assistance or help from people at the church and I had far surpassed my physical capabilities. The following day, I called a friend that lived out of town but owned a house in Tuscaloosa and she allowed me to stay there for one full week. I had packed enough clothes in suitcases to last for several weeks and had thrown a few last minute articles into the car that the movers had left behind. Overwhelmed with gratitude and exhaustion, a solitary place to recover undisturbed for several days satisfied my greatest need. The only necessity that the house lacked was a bathmat which ironically was the last item I had tossed in the trunk of my car because the movers missed packing it. I lacked for nothing. God was covering every detail, even the bathmat.

When I moved in spring 2010, I was 49 years old, 5'6" tall weighing 118 pounds which I had not seen on any scale since my high school days. The circumstances beginning in October 2009 to that point in April 2010 had depleted me of all strength, appetite and the ability to make clear decisions. Despite my circumstances but also because of them, I needed a job and was fortunate to have another family friend that owned a real estate company that gave me an office and a place to get started. It was truly a gift and an opportunity for which I will always be grateful. The other miraculous event was that a friend of my mother's had a single daughter that was my age and sight unseen, allowed me to stay with her and live in her beautiful condominium overlooking the city. She never asked me for a dime and this by itself was nothing short of a miracle because a dime was about all that I had at that time. God had protected me from moving into that home up by the lake and actually opened a door of grace to a place far better. Heather, a single mother, was working in an executive position in Birmingham but living in Tuscaloosa. She had raised a beautiful daughter that had moved to NYC to attend college. Heather and I became instant friends. During that time, she and her former college boyfriend reconnected on Facebook. He was a native of a Middle Eastern country that had returned home following his college experience at Alabama and was now a business owner. They traveled to meet each other as often as possible, despite the great distance.

In October 2010, my paid in advance, Birmingham-blessing condominium tenant elected to move out to minimize her expenses. This allowed me to repay Heather by swapping condominiums, she living in mine and me in hers. My investment condominium was only 5 minutes from her job. Again, this was a wonderful scenario that only the Lord could have orchestrated. Eventually, my new friend and her boyfriend decided it was time to be in one city and she moved to be with him and her daughter returned back into their condominium for the summer signaling the close of this season. I will be forever grateful to Heather for this magnanimous act of kindness towards me.

In late May of 2010, I had lived in Tuscaloosa only less than a month when it became apparent that serving in this local fellowship setting was not going to be God's plan for me in that city. He knew that I would have never left Birmingham had I understood that His plan would entail leaving my church so He used the church to get me to His city then switched the plan. Jehovah S'Nikki! A prayer leader at the main church campus was contacted and I asked permission to teach the prayer training class over the summer, as it was normally only offered in the spring or fall due to its length. I trained a small team of intercessors to be the support beams for that local fellowship with a 12 week prayer course that was retrofitted into 8 weeks. Teaching a closely knit intercessory prayer team while remaining silent on my intention to leave was a grueling and highly emotional experience.

Intercessors have a very unique bond that is spiritual – one can feel it in their soul when someone is missing from the team. I cared for them deeply as friends and co-laborers in Christ, and complicating matters I was leaving the only friends at the time that I had in Tuscaloosa. Each class I poured everything that I had ever learned about prayer into these student intercessors, citing multiple examples from great teachers on prayer that had caught my attention over the years. I taught these intercessors as if that class would be the very last class I would ever teach and then quietly left the church. No one knew – there was no great weepy public announcement, I just simply stopped attending. After 8 years, faded away, and all the while privately virtually crying a river over the realization that I would be leaving but did know clearly that God was pulling me out of this local campus.

Completely wrung out, I was exhausted from the entire ordeal surrounding my exit from Birmingham, the move itself and all of the accompanying uncertainties of being in a city where God wanted me but being unsure why. Anxiously, I waited for Him to show me where He wanted to place me in my next church family. I connected with a group of powerful city Intercessors from a variety of churches that met once per week that could pray the paint off of any wall. We petitioned God for all manner of things and anything that could impact the city; its citizens, churches and pastors, economic growth– everything. The latter, the city's economy, continued to come up for me to cover in prayer over and over again. I consistently sensed that the city was going to need money, a great deal of money for some very important reason that was not discernible, but diligently continued to seek it in prayer.

Throughout this time frame I was still feeling the need to heal and simply gave myself the freedom to not be pressured to quickly re-establish another church membership. I was praying diligently for the Lord's leading and listening to internet sermons and visiting various churches hearing messages, many of which I felt the Lord had scripted just for me during this part of my journey. Tired and disconnected feeling from all of the moving back and forth and now back again in Tuscaloosa, practically everything I owned had been in storage and I lived with only my personal bare necessities for over a year. It would be 14 months from that late April day that I originally moved from Birmingham before my life would return to a sense of normalcy and I had my own place to live again.

During this season, specifically during the initial move into Tuscaloosa, I had several remarkable things happen that came straight from God. Still and to this day, I believe that had I remained in Birmingham, this revelation would not have been imparted to me, one that came directly from the

Holy Spirit.

In August 2010, I had just completed training the core group of the intercessory prayer team and then left the Tuscaloosa church plant, yet still grieving the departure and listening very intently for God's next move. I was in the living room of my friend's condominium, and simply walking across the den, when suddenly and with no warning, an explosive impartation dropped into my spirit. I stopped in my tracks and watched a scene as if on a movie reel, a Technicolor Jesus hanging from the cross, His head dropping. I saw His Spirit leave His body. I somehow knew that He had released and dismissed His own Spirit of His own will and that His life had not been taken from Him. No one person or culture of people had killed Jesus. It then began to be revealed to me by the Spirit that we have been given everything we need in this life because it was all purchased for us at the Cross. This came to me like an impression in my spirit. God was unlocking His treasury and showing me a very great mystery on a divine movie screen.

The understanding that we already own our healing, our provision, our peace, and our sanctification, all through Him, that His body and His blood has paid for everything that we need was coming to me for the first time. I later learned how He became our righteousness and made us to be righteous in the sight of God. (Romans 3:22-26) We need only walk with expectation in receiving these benefits. Our only requirement is to pray, be diligent, rest and have faith in Him. I could not believe what I was seeing in the spirit – and had never heard this taught before nor thought that

I had ever read anything like this in the bible. I had never been reading the bible through the lens of grace!

One evening later, I did something I never do – fall asleep on the sofa. At midnight, on the dot, I was awakened by the Holy Spirit to see on the television screen a thin Asian man in a white jacket and white slacks named Joseph Prince at the very beginning of his broadcast message. I had never heard of him but listened very intently knowing it was not accidental that this was occurring. Amazingly even miraculously, Pastor Prince was teaching on the finished work of the cross, exactly what the Lord had shown me earlier! It was obvious to me that God wanted me to hear this confirmation. I sat straight up on the sofa – transfixed by what I was hearing, knowing this was from God because of the timing with which I was watching this Joseph Prince segment. Had watching this telecast occurred prior to my downloaded revelation on the Finished Work from the Holy Spirit, I would have simply dismissed what I received as something that I had heard from Pastor Prince. God knew how to reveal His confirmation to me in a way that I fully understood what He was doing.

When the segment was over, I turned on my computer to find out who this man was and to learn more about his ministry. I did not know what to do with this revelation but knew it was brought straight to me from the throne room of God. I had no church, few friends and was not in ministry service but this revelation had been imparted to me by God, with no question in my mind. Totally unsure what to do with the information, after several months, I began to post articles on what I was learning and also identified with two other pastors, aside from Joseph Prince, that had had this same revelation so I could be taught by them; Creflo Dollar and Andrew Wommack. This entire book could have been devoted to the topic of the Gospel of grace and the finished work of the cross.

PERSPECTIVE

Since that revelation in 2010, it has been a remarkable journey of discovery through the rich treasuries of the mystery of the sacrifice of Jesus, the blood of Jesus and the existence of the Eternal Covenant made between Jesus and God on our behalf. The authority that has been given to us by God through the sacrifice of His Son is mind boggling on a human scale. We owe everything to Jesus, absolutely everything. What has been imparted to us by having the Holy Spirit live within us is like having our own personal GPS system hardwired in to our souls. He is our advocate, our teacher, comforter, counselor, wisdom-giver, favor imparter – you name it, He does it. Holy Spirit administrates all of the gifts given to us by God as well as coordinates our lives to receive the benefits promised to us by God through Abraham, as were given to him in the book of Genesis. Abraham is the Father of our Faith. He had great favor with God because his own faith was counted to him as righteousness. (Genesis 15:6)

The New Covenant presents Jesus Christ as High Priest (Hebrews 9:15-28) and King (Revelation 17:14), and one who took every sin from the beginning of time to the very end, so that He stands as our righteousness before God – we can never earn righteousness through our works or good behavior, we must only look to Jesus who transforms us in His likeness from glory to glory. This is the Gospel of grace message – everything effectively flows to and through Jesus, never our own performance or sin-conscious behavior.

I am confident, as incredibly painful as it was, that God pulled me out from my previous fellowship so that the Holy Spirit could train me Himself in a new and fresh way of understanding the New Covenant, Jesus and His finished work, as well as to instruct me in essential New Covenant based principles of prayer and healing.

Chapter Eight

The Perfect Storm

During this period, I was working on several projects as a consultant after quickly seeing that the move to real estate was premature in an unknown market. When Heather moved back to Tuscaloosa in preparation for her move overseas, I returned to Birmingham to market and sell my condominium. I had been back in the Birmingham condominium for 4 weeks when on April 25, 2011 the weather forecasters began to mention a "perfect storm" of weather conditions that were on a collision course over our viewing area.

By the afternoon of April 26, schools had chosen to close earlier the following day. At 6:30 AM, April 27th, I awoke to a drip, drip, dripping sound as water was bouncing off the back of my sofa. Not once in 6 years of ownership, had I ever experienced a problem with leaking even though the condominium was a penthouse unit. Straight line winds were cutting across the building, driving raindrops turned rain daggers into every crack and crevice on the roof. Grabbing a towel, I hopped up onto the back of the sofa to dab at the water that was pouring through my crown molding onto my painting when from across the room, I heard my television turn on. I had been watching the water on the ceiling and the television had definitely been off and I had been asleep just moments prior. When it turned on, I quickly turned my head and noticed the remote was located securely on the table by the television and I was standing on the sofa which was halfway across the room. The television had supernaturally turned on without me touching it.

Stunned, I turned around and stared in awe as the face of a young evangelist, Nick Vujicic, appeared on the screen. He was explaining a scenario where he had been enrolled by parents to counsel high school students that were engaging in wrongful actions – as he was recounting the conversation with these parents, he looked right into the camera and spoke these words 3x, "Everything is going to be alright, everything is going to be alright, everything is going to be alright". I stood on the back of the sofa with water pouring through the crown molding, mouth open and eyes wide, in complete disbelief at the supernatural occurrence that I was living. Little did I know that I was going to need each one of these "everything is going to be alrights" more than I could have even imagined.

By 2:00 PM, the Birmingham city schools had closed and the weather forecasters had put its viewing area on its highest possible alert tracking the storms coming from the west as they entered into the state. Tornados were moving straight toward downtown Birmingham and my condominium building was in the trajectory of the tornado's path. When the storms went into warning status, I nervously rode the elevator down into the parking garage, walked to my car and turned on the car radio to listen to the meteorologist's play by play. As the storm continued to get closer and closer to my high-rise, I watched the trees outside in the park rock back and forth as the wind continued to blow stronger and stronger. Aloud and alone in my car, I began to pray very strongly, and at times in my prayer language but most of the time by faith applying the blood of Jesus to myself, and all of my family and our Tuscaloosa property.

Father I ask for the precious blood of Jesus to cover me, this building, the people living here and all of its contents and in Tuscaloosa my family (naming them) and our homes and businesses-thank you for your protective covering. You Lord are Jehovah Nissi our protector and defender.

Following the passing of the storms, I was ecstatic to learn that my family did not lose even one tree or brick from any of their property everyone was completely spared. Unfortunately, 12% of Tuscaloosa and most of the community of Holt were completely demolished, the majority of the devastation localized in the poorest sections of Tuscaloosa and conversely, also at the highest density commercial intersection. Somehow the shopping centers on two corners of the intersection were largely spared but the storm took out three freestanding businesses and an entire subdivision of homes on the opposite corners of the intersection. One fact has always been intriguing – 71% of the storm's trajectory strategically destroyed lower end rental property, and community housing projects. God did not send this tornado, this was a work from the devil, but I do know that impoverished conditions grieve God's heart. It would not surprise me if He modified the trajectory of this storm to remove these decayed areas to be rebuilt with more caring conditions in mind. This in fact has been the result of this clearing away with newly constructed affordable housing communities now replacing projects in dire need of repair. While I was in the parking garage praying as the storm was passing, somehow my dad was able to connect to me from his cell phone after the storm had already ripped through Tuscaloosa. No one was leaving their homes yet so he had no idea of the devastation that would await him when he could get out of his neighborhood and crossed over the Black Warrior River. He called to check and to make sure I had gotten myself off of the 10th Floor. I was the only one that had left the 10th floor, or the 9th floor or even the 8th floor, as no one else was down in the parking garage but me. After I stopped praying and the storm blew through, I returned to my condo but the television signal was out. Releasing mass email distributions to my address book of friends seemed to be the best way to let people know that we were all alive and that no one had been hurt. People were watching the news reports streaming through on their local channels across the state and throughout the United States. I began receiving phone calls from well - wishing friends which was a great source of comfort. I still remember the first call I received – a dear friend from Mobile. When the television signal reconnected and the footage from Tuscaloosa began, it was devastating and beyond anything that could have been imagined. The only way to describe the scene was that it resembled the detonation of powerful bombs around very large sections of the city, leveling every home and tree for great distances and in some cases miles. I cried for hours after seeing the footage of the devastation.

The storm's original path headed up from south of the city and was making a straight line to the University of Alabama campus. Miraculously, it turned away from campus, taking a sharp 90 degree turn, heading into the West End of town where it vaporized the Rosedale Housing Project and several older, historic neighborhoods. The Rosedale housing project, owned and managed by the Tuscaloosa Housing Authority, had been earmarked for demolition for the upcoming fall – the tornado simply accelerated its demise by several months, one of the few good things that came from the initial fall-out of the storm but regardless a terrible tragedy as many of its residents were older and now displaced with few options for shelter.

For many obvious reasons, it was critical that the storm's trajectory bypass the University of Alabama campus. The storm was timed the week prior to final exams, more commonly known as "Dead Week". Most of the students were in the libraries or in buildings or dorms studying, with no attention being paid to weather conditions until then U of A President Robert Witt got on the loudspeaker and directed them to move to a place of protection. Of the 52 people that lost their lives in that tragic tornado, 6 of the dead were University of Alabama students that were off campus for one reason or another. There is no way to ever know what the total fatality number would be if the storm had not taken that 90 degree turn away from campus. One half mile north of campus, the storm also bypassed DCH Regional Medical Center, the third largest hospital in the state but plowed through a historic neighborhood just across the highway from the hospital. There is little doubt that the result could have been anything less than catastrophic had the path not veered to avoid the hospital.

The day after the tornado struck, and against the better

judgment of several people, I took the one hour drive south to Tuscaloosa to view the devastation first hand. There were and still are no words for what I witnessed that day and many days, into months following April 27, 2011 when nothing but rubble and devastation could be seen for miles in certain large sections of the city. After visually confirming that all of my family was safe and their property was secure, I drove over to the West End of town. Driving closer to the devastation, traffic was being re-routed but I looked up and saw two pastor friends and West End / Rosedale Hope Initiative team members; Pastor Larry Doughty of Jesus Way and Pastor Mike Paciello, Pillars of Reconciliation, walking towards what had been the Rosedale Housing community. I picked them up and we were allowed to drive through the police roadblocks and get closer to the scene because we were associated with this community initiative. Again, there are few words to describe what we witnessed when we arrived at Rosedale. Most of the buildings had been vaporized yet people were picking through the rubble, trying to find anything they could that would be of some use. The scene was heart wrenching to watch. People were stumbling around in complete shock, traumatized from losing everything they owned. The directors of the Tuscaloosa Housing Authority, who were on our team, were in full operation, working frantically to place the residents into alternative housing and getting counts of residents to see who needed to be counted among the missing.

The Salvation Army Church and Homeless Shelter also located in the West End and just down from Rosedale, had been completely blown from its foundation, leaving the city with no shelter to house the throngs of people that were left to roam the streets that could not afford hotel rooms nor had family to house them. This high level of displacement went on for weeks and weeks. It is suspected there still may be colonies of homeless living in the woods and other places around the city that require shelter yet still have few places to turn as the Salvation Army buildings were under insured. Five years later and with new leadership at the helm, the Salvation Army's shelter is reaching its funding goal and rebuilding the community shelter.

As the Communications Coordinator of the Rosedale - West End Hope Initiative team, I emailed a request for an emergency meeting. We assembled together at Calvary Church on April 28th to formulate a crisis management plan that could assist our zone of the city. Calvary coordinated an elaborate and very effective drive-thru collection point in their parking lot for household items, packaged food and baby care needs. Several members of the team, comprised of many pastors, went door to door with chain saws, cutting trees off homes and cars and insuring that people had the necessary supplies to attend to their daily survival. The communication was managed to match needs with available community resource services. We all worked at a very fast pace for many weeks. The churches were on the frontline of the entire recovery effort and instrumental in saving the city of Tuscaloosa. The Lord was so gracious to allow me in Tuscaloosa during this time as I was able to witness firsthand the power of the hands and feet of the body of Christ at work. Church members from all denominations came together from every direction working to help their own and everyone in need within their reach. The churches in this Alabama town had never been more unified as the Body served together in unity and with singular focus: to save people and property. The churches of Tuscaloosa and out of town churches that sent aid, resources and people into the city dramatically lightened the financial load for city and federal government agencies, well into the many millions of dollars. Samaritan's Purse, and World Vision maintained active outposts in Tuscaloosa for at least a year and a half past the initial devastation donating hundreds of thousands of dollars of aid to people in need.

I witnessed first-hand the need for every city in America to develop a crisis management action plan which properly and efficiently integrates the sectors of city government, ministry and business marketplace leaders well in advance of a natural disaster. The local church became a one stop shopping destination for disaster recovery, activating as miniature City Halls armed with the capability of (1) quick financial disbursement to numerous lines of resource distribution, (2) marshaling an army of volunteers who work in a long list of secular vocations from which the church can draw expertise and resources, (3) leveraging a closely held authority structure that can pass on instruction through channels of people to get tasks accomplished efficiently, and lastly, (4) having existing lines of communication that allow for swift distribution of information.

It is safe to say that a natural disaster will be coming to your city or a city near you when you least expect it. The local church is the key component to every community's successful crisis management strategic plan.

As an Intercessor, I do believe that this storm was the reason that God placed on my heart a sense of urgency to pray in faith in advance to strengthen economic resources and growth for Tuscaloosa. The expense of digging out of such a catastrophe is overwhelming and monumental for any city. Often I have wondered if prayer is the only thing that moves the hand of God because of the untold number of times that I have prayed for something for which I had little understanding or prayed for someone that I did not personally know because the Lord placed them on my heart – cannot God move without us asking Him? Surely so, but I believe that He wants us to petition Him in faith and obedience if we hear His voice to move in prayer for an individual or even a city, or our nation. There is no doubt in my mind that the trajectory of the Tuscaloosa tornado averting the University of Alabama campus and the state's third largest regional hospital was because of the power of prayer. There is really no other explanation based on its tracking and positioning, this was simply a miracle that occurred purely by the grace of God.

There is story after story of people narrowly escaping death through miraculous means. One non-denominational Tuscaloosa County church in the community of Holt was completely spared when everything around it on all sides was leveled flat for a mile – not a tree or a shrub left in the ground. That church and its young pastor became a hub of hope for the entire community and a point of distribution for food and clothing. There were numerous pastors in the severely impacted community of Holt that worked day and night at the expense of their own health, to stabilize and return it back to a degree of municipal normalcy.

It did not go unnoticed to me that God brought me back to this community in the same timing as the April 27th tornado. Unless you have ever experienced a catastrophic natural disaster, it is difficult to describe what happens within an impacted community. I am grateful for this experience and having the opportunity to watch the church in full action – this was the Body working at its finest. A short while following this disaster, I wrote and published a blog post that describes my observations following this tragic tornado.

PERSPECTIVE

EQUIP THE BRIDE May 23, 2011

Tuscaloosa, Alabama – I have watched for weeks as churches put forth Herculean effort to resource and rescue thousands of Tuscaloosa citizens in the wake of one of the most devastating storms in our country's history. Still The Body functions in excellence. This week, a meeting of 40 Tuscaloosa pastors met for a time of unified, corporate prayer to seek God's wisdom for each other, their congregations and the city. The wisdom of God will be a strong requirement to move forward with vision and fortitude in the months, and likely years, ahead.

Each day I observe the undeniable need for funding the local church as we become increasingly aware of these organizations as powerful centralized distribution hubs for stability, resource and counsel. Churches, like mini City Halls, possess the infrastructure for financial disbursement and accountability, the ability to provide clothing, food and shelter, stability and healing as well as serving as points of access for connection to every conceivable vocation through its members. Churches are the finest "one stop shopping" option for disaster relief. In the days ahead, all churches will be utilized more frequently as access hubs for immediate stabilization, healing and disbursement of resources but first they themselves must be properly structured and resourced. This is serious, time-sensitive business.

> "So Pharaoh asked them, 'Can we find anyone like this man, one in whom is the Spirit of God?'"
> -Genesis 41:38

Pharaoh of course was referring to Joseph. This is the hour for marketplace Joseph's to stand in preparation and walk in action to equip, fund and structure the Church, the bride of Christ, in anticipation of His return and enable Her to stand uprightly and majestically within every community served. (Not merely have Her stand with the aid of a cane or a walker – but properly financially resourced to function in full capacity.)

The need for funding has never been greater for churches and ministries in Tuscaloosa, Alabama. I am writing to simply sound the alarm because of what I see happening. The anointing is here, the people and hearts are here but it is time to move and equip these Brides. Do not let the Bride go hungry (without food banks), dress shabbily (without clothes closets) or be in ill health (without health centers) or become in disrepair. Do not let the Bride become inadequately staffed and forced to turn from people who require healing and wise counsel – the type of counsel that is imparted from the wise and Godly as they hear from the Spirit of God.

> *"But it is the spirit in a man, the breath of the Almighty, that gives Him understanding"*
> -Job 32:8

Equip the Bride and Her Children, para-church ministries that are not churches. Do not make them beg for discernment of their worth if you know they are set apart by God for His work and purposes. Tuscaloosa is no different from any other community – disaster will come to a city near you – each Bride in each community needs to be equipped and structured.

It is the responsibility of the Church through The Body to equip, educate and counsel people on El Shaddai (God Almighty, All Sufficient One, Genesis 17:1)and the meaning of the covenant, redemptive names purchased through the exchange at the cross and Jesus' blood sacrifice which covers the scope of every human need : Shammah (His Presence, Ezekiel 48:35), Shalom (Peace, Judges 6:24), Ra-ah (Shepherd / Pastor, Psalm 23:1), Jireh (Provision,

Genesis 22:14), Nisi, (Banner of Victory over principalities and darkness, Exodus 17:15), Righteousness (Tsidkenu, Jeremiah 23:6), Rapha (Healer, Exodus 15:26), and Jehovah M'Kaddesh (Sanctifier, Leviticus 20:8). A tremendous responsibility indeed but one in which The Church, the Bride of Christ is uniquely designed to deliver but must be adequately enabled to perform. Simply put, please give money to the churches, they will soon be serving entire cities, not just their own membership rolls.

The city lost 21 churches plus the Salvation Army buildings. Please pray for those people who have lost their places of worship, fellowship, resource and community. Thank you for your continued prayers that city and state government leadership and spiritual leadership hear from the spirit of God.

Chapter Nine

It is God's Will for You to Prosper

In March 2011, still living in Birmingham, I received a phone call from a woman that had seen my condominium listing for sale on the internet. As I was sitting in Birmingham she was in, of all places, Tuscaloosa. She drove up to look at it then made a workable offer within two weeks. This of course allowed me to return back to Tuscaloosa with no real estate or financial ties to Birmingham. God has His seasons and His reasons on His timing but it worked out that they allowed me to live there for some time following the tornado because the housing inventory in the city was so depleted.

The first fourteen months of returning back to Tuscaloosa was met with one extreme challenge after another – if an F4 tornado destroying a large part of my new city was not enough, job hiring and available housing came to a screeching halt all across the city as everyone went into survival mode. Upon arriving, I needed an immediate income source and had started out in real estate but was getting little traction. I had returned to Birmingham to sell my condominium with no place to live in Tuscaloosa and still no full-time employment following its sale and now dealing with a severely damaged and literally "torn up" city. All of my belongings had been in storage since April 2010. On June 1, 2011, 14 months after moving to Tuscaloosa, I was able to move all of my belongings out of storage and into a beautiful home. Once again God had handled every important detail on my behalf. I walked into that house for the first time and burst into tears – it was the ideal square footage and was actually a better fit for me than my Birmingham home. God through my earthly father had provided for another primary need. My furniture fit perfectly, as if the home was fashioned by God just for me.

Several months after moving into my house a temporary job opportunity arose in Huntsville, where my lodging and all expenses were paid. The salary was nothing to boast about, but it did satisfy several primary needs so I accepted it despite the inconvenience of living 3 hours from Tuscaloosa during the week. After 3 months, the temporary position ended and I returned unsure of where I would find a job from that point. Five days after returning home, a family friend owning a prime restaurant location called and asked me to list and lease the property on his behalf – again a notable grace door opening from God where I could take no credit. The afternoon that the listing agreement was signed, I placed one call to a client with whom I had been persisting for well over a year prior; persuading them that the timing was now ideal to open their restaurant concept in our market. They had missed this same location once before. That very afternoon, the owner sent his son down to see the site. It took many months to close but did. I was extremely grateful that God extended his hand of provision to me so quickly, re-opening this door in real estate, and allowing a previous sown seed to become harvested at a much needed time.

There have been multiple grace doors that have opened that brought provision across my path in unusual and at times miraculous ways. The Godly principle of seed time and harvest is a very real principle of provision for God's kingdom. In October 2012, I was watching my favorite television network, TBN, as they were hosting their bi-annual fundraising telethon. Every fall and every spring TBN holds a fundraising campaign that lasts for at least 2-3 weeks and has done so for their 40 year existence. As a partner, I had sent money to TBN for several years but paid no special attention to these telethons however this one happened to have several of my favorite teaching pastors participating in the event so I listened with renewed interest. It was impossible to ignore the strong anointing flowing from these teachers as they were speaking on a particular word given to them by the Lord. One morning during this campaign, a teacher began to speak that I had never watched on TBN before but he caught my attention because he worked in a financial career for many years before becoming a pastor. He continued to teach on sowing seeds – teachings that I had heard before but paid little attention to in the past.

As he continued to speak, his words began to make more and more sense to me. He then specifically mentioned real estate transactions which really caught my interest. Although not intending to open up my wallet over what I was hearing, he made another mention that a real estate transaction was getting blessed so I thought, "Why not?" and had a specific dollar amount in mind that I would send simply to try this out. The pastor then requested a higher specific dollar amount than what I was considering that would protect that seed for one full year. It was still not much but it was more than I had or wanted to give. As he was speaking I kept walking closer and closer to the television, which I never do. As God is my witness, He knew I did not want to give that higher amount but I felt the Holy Spirit prompt me noticeably and extremely hard! My mouth dropped I grabbed my stomach and thought I would faint before I could grab the phone and make that call. I made that pledge so fast - eyes would spin out of any head. I dove for that phone and would have given twice the amount after the Lord gave me that "hint". I paid the invoice when it arrived then honestly thought little more about it.

That very same month and about 2 weeks later, I was driving through town and passed a large parcel of property that I had driven past thousands of times and for some reason in late October 2012, this property looked just a little different that day. I pulled up the tax records then ran off some information then called a friend in Atlanta and asked if he might know anyone that might be interested in purchasing property adjacent to the University. I then called the leasing agent on the property and he said that the property was not on the market which I already knew but confirmed that it was 5 acres. He informed me that the last price offered on the property from a group out of Texas was $4.5 million and the ownership turned it down. I thanked him for the information then called my Atlanta contact and told him that the property price would be $5 million and it was 3 blocks from the stadium and the freshman dorms, situated on a major city thoroughfare with very high traffic counts. After sending him several additional documents I then waited, November and December came and went, as did

January and then part of February I had reasoned that the possibility was dead by this point.

In late February, the founder of a student housing development company called and said that he was not only interested, but that he wanted to purchase the property. I contacted the owners directly and explained that an offer was going to be made. For the next 6 months, every conceivable obstacle began to occur making it appear that this transaction would not go through to a closing. Articles written in the newspaper, a Task Force established by the Mayor to study the existing housing inventory, retail businesses located in the center were writing letters to the Editor of the paper – backlash from the community was in abundant supply.

Throughout the process, particularly toward the end, I would continue to speak in power that the seed sown would surround the transaction like an anchor of protection just as had been promised prophetically. When my faith waned, I would speak out loud that, "I am the righteousness of God by faith in Christ Jesus" and that "No weapon formed against my financial prosperity will prosper". In my daily time of worship with Jesus, I would thank Him that His sacrifice opened the door to every blessing promised to Abraham and that I was a child of the Eternal Covenant and God's Beloved. These declarations kept my faith up and my mouth shut to negative self-talk, both of which are crucial for faith and winning with God. I would also remind myself continually of the love that God has for me and that He was working on my behalf for this transaction to come to fruition.

Finally, just 3 weeks shy of one year to the day that I sowed that seed and made that ministry donation, the property transaction closed, and was the highest sales price per acre ever recorded in the county. Granted, it was an incredible piece of property. I celebrated by sowing seed right back into the Kingdom, and into some of my favorite ministries which brought me great joy. Kingdom ministries must be funded by Christians – over and above non ministry not-for-profit organizations. Our local churches and para-church ministries must be fully funded enabling them to perform at their highest levels in these last days. God's word states that He will rebuke the devourer for our sake, if we tithe to His church. Anything over the 10%; 11% and over, is considered an offering to God and will be blessed at 30, 60, 100 fold return. My low 3 figure seed offering yielded a $103,000 commission with a "blessing" rate of return at 3,760 times more than the original seed. My very first commercial real estate sale was $5.1 million. Now that's my kind of investment strategy! Maybe only a wildly popular tech stock purchased right at a company start up could have this rate of return. Give me a safe - bet "Kingdom tip" from the Holy Spirit any day. The Holy Spirit ordered my steps to intersect with people and circumstances that blessed me in ways I could have never planned on my own. This was all made possible only by Him.

PERSPECTIVE

I love this testimony more than just the obvious reason that I benefitted financially from a large transaction. "Leading a believer to the mouth of the fish" is what the Holy Spirit wants to do for us and how He wanted to do it for me in this instance. When we have a clear understanding of true grace, we know that we are to live life by the promptings of the Spirit and doing so requires an uncommon relationship with God, the Father, Jesus and Holy Spirit. You must be in step with what they are telling us and be prepared to do what they ask us to do. Many tests occur along the way. I have been awakened by God in the middle of the night many times, and being drawn out of a very deep sleep to hear a teaching or be given a thought that the Lord wanted communicated to others or that He simply wanted me to understand. Multiple times in the middle of the night my television turned on supernaturally so that I would be given confirmation on a word that the Lord had given me on a topic on which I had written because in this way, I would know without a doubt that the confirmation was from Him.

There have been times that I wondered why He would want to use me. There is nothing extraordinary about me, actually, just the opposite is true. He does know that I care deeply for His Son and the knowledge of His blood and what it can do for all people. I have jokingly, privately referred to myself as The Blood "guinea pig", as I have experienced certain seasons of trial and testing that have brought me to the very edge yet learning to take each promise of the covenant names of God, working through them using the sacrifice of Jesus as my framework. For example, Shalom His Peace, is given to us as a gift based on the sacrifice so I picture my mind calibrated to the mind of Jesus and through the blood of His sacrifice and His name, I take authority over my mind, making a demand on the covenant for the peace that was purchased. I then ask the Spirit to move and to remove every spirit that is not from the Spirit of God, and place the mind of Jesus into my own. I also work towards specifically binding spirits that I can identify that are attacking my peace.

Over time, I have taken each primary promise: health, provision, peace, protection, God's presence, righteousness and have fashioned for myself prayers that incorporate the blood, the name of Jesus and the Spirit. Doing this plus the revealed knowledge of true grace has helped me triumph over many a trial.

Chapter Ten

Mercy Triumphs over Judgment

Despite a late start in accepting Jesus, I can now say that the extremely difficult circumstances surrounding my marriage were directly responsible for saving my soul from becoming eternally lost. Prior to this experience I was a hard case, not bad or immoral, but lukewarm, somewhat self-righteous and most importantly unknown to me despite consistent church attendance, not secure in going to Heaven. By stepping out onto a road less traveled based on a series of circumstances hallmarked by rejection, God opened a doorway of grace during a very murky and disappointing season. My life and mind were opened into a new realm of possibility and way of living that I may never have known existed. Before my ministry experience, I was convinced that attending church one Sunday a week coupled with believing that Jesus was God's Son were the only two necessary keys to gaining entrance into heaven but there is more, much more.

> *8 But what does it say? "The word is near you; it is in your mouth and in your heart that is the word of faith that we are proclaiming. 9 That if you confess with your mouth, "Jesus is Lord," and believe in your heart that God raised Him from the dead, you will be saved. 10 For it is with your heart that you believe and are justified, and it is with your mouth that you confess and are saved.*
> -Romans 10:8-10

God has been so merciful to me over a 15 year period to bring forth apostolic pastor-shepherds / teachers and divine counsel from His Holy Spirit. He has been so gracious to give me hopeful experiences and glimpses of Himself and the love that He has for all of us in very tangible ways.

To state that Jesus was raised from the dead, or resurrected, means of course that He is still alive. Why would God need Jesus to remain alive? Wasn't what Jesus did enough? He is alive because He still has a purpose for living! Jesus intercedes for us day and night to the Father, as our High Priest and the Mediator of the Eternal Covenant. Jesus takes our confession (our need) and through Him when professed with faith, our requests become a reality. Jesus petitions on our behalf to God for all things. Acknowledge that He has already paid the price for your prosperity, finances, peace and to be protected and then thank Him for it.

When teaching the gospel or Good News of Jesus, I am purposeful about explaining Jesus' role as the great High Priest discussed in Hebrews 10. Jesus is not only alive and seated next to God but His blood and its power are still very much alive as well. Jesus' blood is the most powerful substance given to us on this earth and when applied to a situation or circumstance and combined with an unshakeable degree of faith, you can own His power yourself. I have learned that a sure way to God's heart and His throne room is to accept and understand that there was a very high price paid for the redemption of every person and it was by the blood of His Son.

For a person to acknowledge that Jesus paid sin debt by

becoming a sacrifice of His own will because only He as the sin-less Deity could be used shows that (1) a person understands that they cannot get to Heaven by their own skill, performance or even avoidance of sin, and (2) they understand that their sins were not merely atoned for, which means "covered over", but they were redeemed or purchased and bought back. An exchange physically took place within Jesus' own body for us while He hung on the cross. All the sin of humanity was imputed unto Jesus.

> *See, my servant will act wisely; He will be raised and lifted and highly exalted. 14 Just as there were many who were appalled at Him, His appearance was so disfigured beyond that of any man and His form marred beyond human likeness.*
> Isaiah 52:13

His raising by the Holy Spirit or resurrection serves as ratification of this New Covenant made between Jesus and God on our behalf, a radical covenant reality that we can now access through and because of His grace. When one grasps this truth – it acts as a springboard of love towards God and Jesus, birthing a desire to be in their Presence (they are seated side by side in heaven) and to learn more of their ways and a will to build their Kingdom on earth. Our daily life is a discovery of just how forgiven we truly are! We have been cleansed, purged, once and for all of all sin debt past, present and future by the holy blood of the Son of God, and Savior Jesus Christ.

If one clearly understands who Jesus is and what He did,

there is no fear of God and no threat of retribution in fact — it's a "want to" and not a "have to" experience to walk with Him. Once a person makes the decision to accept Christ, they are no longer considered "Sinners" and are now clothed in the garment of a Saint as a Son or Daughter of the living God! And if that is not enough, the Spirit of God then takes up residence within them, becoming the Believer's best friend and closest ally. You are His Beloved and He cares for you with a deep ocean of love. It is easy to take this for granted but we must all stop and truly meditate on the reality of the magnitude that the Creator of the Universe knows you by name and is personally working out situations and circumstances on your behalf— it does not mean everything is easy, and that everything that happens to you in life is grand, but in the end, you can trust that God will bring you around to something that is all very good and that He loves you. If you hold to God's promises, keep your cool and allow Him to work things out on your behalf, you stay "within the blood" and within His own protection and defenses. It is such a comfort to look back and realize how God has been there with me for so much of my life before I accepted His Son. My Abba Daddy saw everything that happened, and made all things work together, because of His love for me, the love I have for His Son and that I honor and esteem His Holy Spirit.

I can also say with great clarity and conviction that my decision to obey God and return home was the very best choice. We all know in our natural minds that God knows best but it's in the walking out of His desires where we can get overly analytical and fearful and dig into people and places that we love but that are just simply not His highest or best. We should always wait for His very best, and trust that He does have one yet I realize that it is much easier to declare that on the other side of the journey! This particular section of the course was a necessary part of my life's walk and a "Big Rock" that needed not be stepped around. My prayer to God has been to never allow me to miss the Big Rocks in my journey that would enable me to get successfully to the other side of where He would want me to be.

PERSPECTIVE

Throughout this entire journey, the Lord shed me of a few close friends and organizations that will apparently not be needed where I am headed. At the time the friendships were dying off, these experiences were extremely painful, even feeling like a real death and a difficult part of my journey. I came to realize that if someone is not a part of the present, they are probably not a part of the future either so I needed to move forward and trust God to bring people into my life that will walk through the marvelous future He has planned and to never look back. Saying this has been easy to embrace would be less than honest.

The first time that this happened, at least the first time that I recognized it for what it was, involved one miscommunicated incident involving a ring, a well-placed close friend managed to successfully turn away most of my inner circle pre B.C. (Before Christian) friends. I made no attempt at defending myself to her or explaining what had actually happened but instead, threw myself into my new full time ministry position. Although my job was situated only 20 minutes north of where most of my friends lived, it was an entire planet's distance away from where most lived at that time spiritually. Had I continued to try to hang onto my B.C. friends while immersing myself in the job through the door that God opened for me, the two together would have never worked and my life would have become confusing. The clean break that I received during this time allowed me to make brand new friends that loved God, and understood His principles. There was nothing socially minded about this church staff, they simply loved Jesus and wanted nothing less than to advance God's Kingdom in excellence. What began as a devastating episode of rejection was used by God to close one door and to open another that was far more beneficial.

Since that time, He has used this same 'tactic' as a way of moving me in a direction that aligns with my life's Strategic Plan crafted by Him. Admittedly, at times, I have wondered if I just neglect to discern His promptings soon enough before a specific season ends and before I have to endure again more of these painful episodes. This tearing away process never seems to get easier but each time one occurs, I have been brought something much greater and more important than where He had me before. We all want a life living among people where we feel celebrated or at least welcomed rather than feeling just barely tolerated. We must always be expectant that God has that special place of contentment. Do not fear letting Him move you based on a need for familiar surroundings. Never settle. God's highest and best may simply be one move away.

Chapter Eleven

It is Finished – Keep your Eyes on Jesus

Over a 15 year period I have had the benefit of "trial by fire" and training by the Holy Spirit. The most important benefits of these experiences pertain to the subject of healing; emotional, deliverance, Holy Spirit guided self-deliverance and self-healing and intercessory prayer. There have been days I would not wish on my worst enemy but God has used each and every one for my benefit. I suppose it would have been a much easier life to have been the wife of an established self-made man, with no need for my own career, to have raised several children while maintaining a lifelong membership in the Junior League (I dropped out in Atlanta), serving at the helm of a number of civic organizations while attending a church one day per week. This was not the life that God planned out for me yet I have had a very exciting and rewarding life. Attending a fine women's college prepared me for many things but nothing that relates to this circuitous route on which God has taken me to meet Him. Writing those long essay questions required to attain that four year liberal arts degree did however teach me something about composition.

The primary reason for writing this book was that I truly believe that time is short before the church is raptured and before Christ's return. The signs in the earth are all around us to substantiate this theory. I realize that this is a sobering comment at the close of what should be a high note in ending this book. We must familiarize ourselves in the ways that God has set out for us to acquire and rest in His covenant benefits of healing, freedom, provision, and peace that are vastly different than ways the world attempts to get there for our own comfort, if not eventual survival. Reading someone's testimony not only brings hope but can light the way. Through all we have nothing to fear. Keeping our eyes fixed on Jesus while never looking to the left or to the right and completely resting in His promises assures us of a secure route.

It is well documented that Jesus' ministry was filled with account after account of healing miracles. We know that Jesus has commissioned us for the work of healing in Mark 16 a chapter which ends in stating that God will be with us and will teach us. Healing must be reclaimed as a major part of every Believer's own personal ministry walk and as a primary function of the Church as a whole. As the days approaching Christ's return become more complex, it is essential that every person that calls on His name understands that they have been given the ability to heal and deliver just as Jesus did in the bible. This gift of healing was also given as one of the benefits in the Eternal Covenant – the same benefits given by God to Abraham as detailed in Genesis.

Throughout my God-journey, and study of Jesus' ministry, I find it interesting that He never had prolonged counseling relationships with anyone He healed. He simply took in information; that He already knew of course, and then bound and or cast out an offending spirit. There was never any long drawn out conversation on His sofa that continued week after week, month after month. No weepy examination of wronged childhoods or tarnished pasts – He was always direct and straight forward, "Rise up and walk – and take your mat too while you are at it." (Paraphrase mine).

In reflecting on my own wonderful counseling experience leading up to and following my divorce, I was in desperate need of wise and confidential counsel and do believe that God sent me the perfect answer in His perfect timing and brought me what I needed in the season in which it was needed. However emotions, fears, and depression following my divorce could have been harnessed more quickly allowing me much needed emotional relief with the knowledge of how to properly pray to bind these emotions. Had I been aware that this was available, this information would have benefitted much more as would have the great grace Gospel news of Jesus that is pouring forth across the world right now. Our real power to free people is by approaching healing just exactly like Jesus did. Every child in God's Kingdom can have a crystal clear understanding of the power of Jesus' blood; what happened to Him and for us from Gethsemane to Golgotha, and the authority we walk in because of the Eternal Covenant by His death and resurrection. We are all designed to have the ability to enlist the Holy Spirit to deliver and heal without the need of another person. The Holy Spirit's power will flow within us and at our disposal so that we can heal and free ourselves. I realize this is radical but I am now a radical healer.

I have walked in divine health for many years however recently have experienced a few tests on my health that could have been potentially severe or fatal. Diagnosed with a very aggressive form of cancer located in a mole on my forearm, I had been praying about this dark mole for several months prior to diagnosis, suspecting that something really did not look right about it yet kept sensing the Holy Spirit telling me to, 'Get it off, get it off, get it off!' I realize that this does not constitute a healing miracle. I did go to a doctor who diagnosed it and he immediately "got it off" within 24 hours following receipt of the lab results. There are those that would consider this as a healing, a warning from the Holy Spirit that was acted upon, avoiding a disastrous outcome. This is a gray area for me but will say that I will take a word from the Holy Spirit when given in any way, shape or form and know that it was for my betterment. I do wish that I would have avoided this nasty scar but fortunately I am still very much alive.

We must remain confident that the work of Jesus was completed at the cross so we remain always standing from a position of victory, never from defeat; begging for provision or healing or whatever it is that we need. Our healing, provision, protection, peace is in the very embodiment of Jesus Himself. His gift to us came through walking out an agreement that was set out for all before the beginning of the world. Healing, provision, protection and peace are provided by and through Jesus and not through our striving. This is difficult to grasp and the fullness of this revelation comes through God's grace. But consider this, if there was any other act or action higher than what Jesus did for us which was to die a traumatic and tormented death – would not the other act be the way that we would achieve

God's blessing on our lives? Why then would it be necessary for Jesus to die? As Jesus Himself said, that once He died there would come a better way – meaning life in the Spirit. One of the most important benefits is that this act of grace allowed for the entrance of the Holy Spirit into those that believe that Jesus is the Son of God and that His blood purchased our redemption. Glory!

> *4 Surely He has borne our grief (sicknesses, weaknesses, and distresses) and carried our sorrows and pains [of punishment], yet we [ignorantly] considered Him stricken, smitten, and afflicted by God [as if with leprosy]. 5 But He was wounded for our transgressions, He was bruised for our guilt and iniquities; the chastisement [needful to obtain] peace and well-being for us was upon Him, and with the stripes [that wounded] Him we are healed and made whole.*
>
> *6 All we like sheep have gone astray, we have turned everyone to his own way; and the Lord has made to light upon Him the guilt and iniquity of us all. 7 He was oppressed, [yet when] He was afflicted, He was submissive and opened not His mouth; like a lamb that is led to the slaughter, and as a sheep before her shearers is dumb, so He opened not His mouth. 8 By oppression and judgment He was taken away; and as for His generation, who among them considered that He was cut off out of the land of the living [stricken to His death] for the transgression of my [Isaiah's] people, to whom the stroke was due? 9 And they*

assigned Him a grave with the wicked, and with a rich man in His death, although He had done no violence, neither was any deceit in His mouth.

10 Yet it was the will of the Lord to bruise Him; He has put Him to grief and made Him sick. When You and He make His life an offering for sin [and He has risen from the dead, in time to come], He shall see His [spiritual] offspring, He shall prolong His days, and the will and pleasure of the Lord shall prosper in His hand. 11 He shall see [the fruit] of the travail of His soul and be satisfied; by His knowledge of Himself [which He possesses and imparts to others] shall My [uncompromisingly] righteous One, My Servant, justify many and make many righteous (upright and in right standing with God), for He shall bear their iniquities and their guilt [with the consequences, says the Lord].

12 Therefore will I divide Him a portion with the great [kings and rulers], and He shall divide the spoil with the mighty, because He poured out His life unto death, and [He let Himself] be regarded as a criminal and be numbered with the transgressors; yet He bore [and took away] the sin of many and made intercession for the transgressors (the rebellious).
- Isaiah 53: 4-12

Faith in the activation of the blood of Jesus, a knowledge in one's authority for healing, an understanding of the grace that God has made available to us, a holy and pure life, accessing the power of the Holy Spirit and God's anointing are all essential ingredients for any healing ministry. Even if someone has other ministry interests, as a Believer, that person has been given the ability and the authority to heal themselves and others. This is powerful and real.

> *Again Jesus went into a synagogue, and a man was there who had one withered hand [[a]as the result of accident or disease]. 2 And [the Pharisees] kept watching Jesus [closely] to see whether He would cure him on the Sabbath, so that they might get a charge to bring against Him [[b]formally]. 3 And He said to the man who had the withered hand, Get up [and stand here] in the midst. 4 And He said to them, Is it lawful and right on the Sabbath to do good or to do evil, to save life or to take it? But they kept silence. 5 And He glanced around at them with vexation and anger, grieved at the hardening of their hearts, and said to the man, Hold out your hand. He held it out, and his hand was [completely] restored. 6 Then the Pharisees went out and immediately held a consultation with the Herodians against Him, how they might [devise some means to] put Him to death.*
>
> *7 And Jesus retired with His disciples to the lake, and a great throng from Galilee followed Him. Also from Judea8 And from Jerusalem and Idumea and from beyond the Jordan and from about Tyre and Sidon—a vast multitude, hearing*

all the many things that He was doing, came to Him. 9 And He told His disciples to have a little boat in [constant] readiness for Him because of the crowd, lest they press hard upon Him and crush Him. 10 For He had healed so many that all who had distressing bodily diseases kept falling upon Him and pressing upon Him in order that they might touch Him. 11 And the spirits, the unclean ones, [c]as often as they might see Him, fell down before Him and kept screaming out, You are the Son of God! 12 And He charged them strictly and severely under penalty again and again that they should not make Him known. 13 And He went up on the hillside and called to Him [[d]for Himself] those whom He wanted and chose, and they came to Him. 14 And He appointed twelve to [e]continue to be with Him, and that He might send them out to preach [as apostles or special messengers] 15 And to have authority and power to heal the sick and to drive out demons: 16 [They were] Simon, and He surnamed [him] Peter; 17 James son of Zebedee and John the brother of James, and He surnamed them Boanerges, that is, Sons of Thunder; 18 And Andrew, and Philip, and Bartholomew (Nathaniel), and Matthew, and Thomas, and James son of Alphaeus, and Thaddaeus (Judas, not Iscariot), and Simon the Cananaean [also called Zelotes], 19 And Judas Iscariot, he who betrayed Him.

20 Then He went to a house [probably Peter's], but

a throng came together again, so that Jesus and His disciples could not even take food.21 And when those [f]who belonged to Him ([g]His kinsmen) heard it, they went out to take Him by force, for they kept saying, He is out of [h]His mind (beside Himself, deranged)!22 And the scribes who came down from Jerusalem said, He is possessed by Beelzebub, and, By [the help of] the prince of demons He is casting out demons.23

And He summoned them to Him and said to them in parables (illustrations or comparisons put beside truths to explain them), How can Satan drive out Satan?24 And if a kingdom is divided and rebelling against itself, that kingdom cannot stand.25 And if a house is divided (split into factions and rebelling) against itself, that house will not be able to last.26 And if Satan has raised an insurrection against himself and is divided, he cannot stand but is [surely]coming to an end.27 But no one can go into a strong man's house and ransack his household goods right and left and seize them as plunder unless he first binds the strong man; then indeed he may [thoroughly] plunder his house.

28 Truly and solemnly I say to you, all sins will be forgiven the sons of men, and whatever abusive and blasphemous things they utter;29 But whoever speaks abusively against or maliciously misrepresents the Holy Spirit can never get forgiveness, but is guilty of and is in the grasp of [i]an everlasting trespass. 30 For they [j]persisted in saying, [k]He has an unclean spirit. 31 Then His mother and His brothers came and, standing outside, they sent word to Him, calling [for] Him. 32 And a crowd was sitting around Him, and they said to Him, Your mother and Your brothers and Your sisters are outside asking for You.

33 And He replied, Who are My mother and My brothers? 34 And looking around on those who sat in a circle about Him, He said, See! Here are My mother and My brothers; 35 For whoever does the things God wills is My brother and sister and mother! -Mark 3: 1-35 AMP

This chapter has many important verses that are useful for the discussion of healing but first a basic lesson. Throughout the bible there are references to spirits; evil spirits, unclean spirits, spirits of fear. For those of you who may be new to the faith, these spirits are common spirits – none holy, and should never be confused with the Spirit of God which is the Holy Spirit. Holy Spirit or "the Spirit" is always denoted with a capital "S" in the bible and as with any title. The Holy Spirit lives inside of each one of us who have a relationship with Jesus. He is a person, not just power, although He is powerful and will give you power. It is the Spirit that administers healing and accomplishes every supernatural act merely flowing through us as a human conduit yielded to God's will. Acts of healing are never done by a human – only through them by God's Holy Spirit with the way paved because of the finished work.

Since my revelation experience several years ago of the finished work, I gratefully have been taught through the bible and a few present day grace teachers the truth regarding God's great love for me, and that all sin past, present and future has been imputed into Jesus, my sin debt to God has been marked PAID and that I am fully accepted by God no matter what because I have accepted His Son. Our sin has been imputed or exchanged for Jesus' righteousness. We must focus on and rest in Jesus to be transformed supernaturally from glory to glory. Condemnation should be quickly identified and replaced with the truth of God's bottomless love which loosens this negative grip and place in our lives. The battle has already been won! The Spirit wields His sword against evil and wills to do so quickly and in His strength, so we enroll Him into the practice by prayer and let Him do it. We understand that these spirits exist but do not ever do so walking in fear, but by resting in Jesus.

In verse 27, Jesus begins speaking in parables to the Pharisees regarding the "strong man". There are categories of demons or "strong men" that rule over a host of associated spirits that can gain access to a person's soul. The following is a <u>partial</u> list of the demon spirits:

  1. Demon spirit of Jealousy

  2. Demon spirit of Lying

3. Familiar spirit

4. Demon spirit of Perversion

5. Demon spirit of Heaviness / Death

6. Demon spirit of Whoredom

7. Demon spirit of Infirmity, Disease and Sickness

8. Demon spirit of Suicide

9. Demon spirit of Fear

While resting and waiting on Jesus to transform a person from glory to glory, it makes the ride more comfortable to bind any offending spirit. Oftentimes I will ask the Holy Spirit to bind these spirits from a person, bringing about healing in their minds or in their bodies quickly. I ask Him to "apprehend every spirit that is not from the spirit of God out from_____'s mind and body". Speak to the Holy Spirit like He is your surgeon, because He is actually doing the surgical work. Identifying and binding spirits is a key principle of delivering oneself and so simple it is almost unbelievable that it truly works. Most people believe that deliverance is for other people but self-deliverance is for all people that have the Holy Spirit in them because again, He is the one that is completing the action. Binding a spirit is not works or performance, it is scriptural. What you bind on earth is bound in heaven.

PERSPECTIVE

If you are going through a season of harsh circumstances; financial problems, uncertainty, health issues, loss – do not lie down and let the devil (spirit of fear, condemnation, etc.) pound you. Rise up and walk my friends, and speak aloud the promises of God while you are walking towards the light. If you are going through a terrible season, identify those spirits that come against you and take Matthew 16:19 AMP as literal truth – that you have been given the Keys to the Kingdom! Enemy #1 is Fear. This is how you, in partnership with the Holy Spirit, can deliver and conquer!

> *"I will give you the keys of the kingdom of heaven; and whatever you bind (declare to be improper and unlawful) on earth must be whatever is already bound in heaven: and whatever you loose (declare lawful) on earth must be what is already loosed in heaven."* Matthew 16:19 AMP

Read also

> *Bind, rebuke and break that spirit by the name of Jesus and by the blood of Jesus Christ. Take your authority. You are blessed with every spiritual blessing in heavenly places.*
>
> -Isaiah 22:22

Prologue

My story is certainly one of redemption, and of grace given to me by a loving Heavenly Father that sought to draw me to Himself from the day of my birth. It has been the greatest joy of life to live saved and free; a Liberty Belle, resting in the assurance that the latter half of my life will be far greater than the first. It is settled that Jesus has completed the course and opened up for me and for you, a life of boundless benefits. This does not guarantee that your life will be a smooth road but He will always make a way through as you strive to create an atmosphere in which His presence enjoys to dwell.

As I complete this book which has taken two years, I have had a few more doors open into a new and exciting season - these are doors that opened by the grace of God and with no initiation on my part. I am convinced now, even more than when I started to write, that God is ever watchful and waiting to open these divine gateways of favor to usher us into seasons of growth, and purpose to fulfill our destinies for His Kingdom. These are doors that cannot be shoved or pushed on, they only come through rest. We must learn to watch for these doors to open, trusting that He knows that we are fully capable of doing what He has opened a door for us to do, and to believe that the door truly opened from Him because of His deep love.

It is my hope that since you have read my story, that you can be confident that you know Jesus better and can have a more active relationship with Him. My greatest wish is that you now know Him and will trust Him with your life and that you will continue to seek Jesus, the Holy Spirit and God your Abba Daddy with everything in you. There is nothing more precious and important than your own personal understanding that you are truly His Beloved.

> *"If you declare with your mouth, "Jesus is Lord", and believe in your heart that God raised him from the dead, you will be saved. For it is with your heart that you believe and are justified, and it is with your mouth that you profess your faith and are saved."* -Romans 10:9-10

Emotional Freedom Prayer

I believe by the fact that you are reading this book, that God is opening a doorway of grace for you. You have the ability to pray for yourself to take action over your emotions and torment that plague your life. The first step is to forgive from your heart, everyone that has wronged you – no matter how deep. Secondly, you need to identify any trauma that has been experienced. This can include: divorce, death, emotional and physical abuse, abandonment, extreme rejection, shame. After you have identified these spirits, forgive the offending parties, and then pray this prayer aloud.

Father, my Abba Daddy, I thank you for your Son, who took every lash and every nail on His body, every thorn in that crown that He wore on His head to purchase healing in my body and peace within my mind. I ask Holy Spirit to apprehend every spirit that is not from the Spirit of God from my mind and I decree and declare that today my mind is calibrated to the perfect shalom peaceful mind of Jesus Christ because He Himself paid for me to own it by His sacrifice. I command all spirits of fear, (name them individually) to release me. You are bound, and broken in the name of Jesus and by the blood of Jesus. I am protected in the Fortress of the Blood of Jesus Christ and you must release me now.

Thank you, Father that I stand in victory and not from defeat in what your Son has done for me through His completed work at Calvary. I am the righteousness of God by faith in Christ Jesus and declare today that no weapon formed against me will prosper. I pray this prayer in the name of Jesus. AMEN (so be it).

www.ingramcontent.com/pod-product-compliance
Lightning Source LLC
Chambersburg PA
CBHW052056070526
44584CB00017B/2200